M000169939

Collins discover

Collins discover

Aquarium
Fish

Don Harper

Collins

An Imprint of HarperCollins*Publishers*

ISBN-10: 0-00-720578-3
ISBN-13: 978-0-00-720578-3

ISBN-10: 0-06-089067-3 (in the United States)
ISBN-13: 978-0-06-089067-4
FIRST U.S. EDITION. Published in 2006.

Created by Toucan Books Ltd.
Author: Don Harper
Editor: Theresa Bebbington
Design: Bradbury and Williams

All photos by Neil Hepworth, except:
Hippocampus-Bildarchiv: 122, 133, 134, 161,
178, 180, 181, 182, 185
Interpet (01306 881 033): 22, 25, 26, 27

Color reproduction by Colourscan, Singapore
Printed and bound by Printing Express Ltd.

10 09 08 07 06
6 5 4 3 2 1

Contents

Your aquarium

Keeping fish for their aesthetic appeal is a pastime that dates back more than one thousand years to ancient Asia. There have been many technological changes during the past century, and these advances have made it easy to set up and maintain an aquarium successfully—no matter where you live.

1 Keeping fish

There are few hobbies that are as relaxing, interesting and enjoyable as keeping an aquarium. You can choose fish with origins from an Amazonian rainforest stream, or you can opt for something more unusual, such as fish that prefer a subterranean cave landscape, the habitat for some of the most bizarre fish in the world. Whichever fish you prefer, you can create different environments for them in your home—where you can gain a unique insight into the natural world of fish.

The appeal of an aquarium

Fish keeping is a hobby offering great scope, whether you want a community aquarium containing a number of different fish, or a setup with only one species. It is not necessarily an expensive hobby, particularly if you concentrate on smaller fish.

An aquarium does not require a large amount of space, and you can easily incorporate one in your home in either an apartment or a house—there are plenty of ways to arrange the decor in a tank to suit your tastes and the needs of the fish. With such a wide range of aquarium fish in an array of shapes and colors, there is certain to be at least one species that will appeal to you—in fact, you might find limiting the choice of the fish for your tank is the most difficult part of keeping fish.

As long as you care for your fish properly, there are a number of fish that you can breed and rear in the home aquarium, adding to the fascination of the hobby. Live-bearers, such as guppies, are generally the most straightforward to breed, while successfully spawning some egg-laying species and rearing their fry can be a real challenge. For the more experienced fish keeper, another possibility is the creation of new color and fin variants, as with angelfish (*Pterophyllum* species) and swordtails (*Xiphophorus* species).

Fish, such as mollies (*Poecilia velifera*), can become so tame that once they recognize you they will readily feed from your hand.

Links with fellow enthusiasts

There can be a social dimension to having an aquarium, with aquatic societies catering both for general fish keepers and also specific groups of fish, such as cichlids. Some of these organizations hold regular meetings, while others operate through the Internet, linking people around the world.

There are also regular fish shows organized by aquatic societies, where fish are exhibited. Specific judging standards have been laid down for a number of the more common aquarium fish, such as goldfish and guppies, which are bred in numerous fancy forms.

Goldfish *(Carassius auratus)* are a wonderful first fish for a child, but do not keep them in a small goldfish bowl. They require a large tank to remain healthy.

The benefits of fish keeping

Scientific investigation into the field of fish keeping has confirmed that watching aquarium fish as they swim around in their tank is a truly relaxing activity. It can lead to a measurable reduction in blood pressure, which brings direct health benefits. This helps to explain why aquaria are often found in potentially stressful localities, such as dentists' waiting rooms.

Furthermore, an aquarium can provide a focal point of interest that can be shared by young and old alike, and a goldfish will make an ideal first pet for a child to look after because it requires minimal adult assistance. Fish keeping is also an activity that can be carried out and greatly enjoyed by those with disabilities who may not be able to care for other pets that require more demanding attention.

weblinks: www.aquahobby.com/e_home.php

Acquiring fish

Fish often differ significantly in their needs and behavior, so it is important to be aware of the requirements of the particular species of fish before you buy any. Otherwise, you are likely to encounter problems when placing them in the tank.

must know

You need to consider the following factors before you buy your fish:
▶ Water chemistry and temperature range
▶ Compatibility
▶ Adult size
▶ Ease of care and breeding
▶ Dietary needs (certain fish have specialist requirements)

White spot is one of the most common diseases to occur in aquarium fish, and it often appears when a fish is subjected to stress. This parasitic infection can provide an entry for fungal infection to strike.

Most aquarium fish are relatively adaptable in terms of their water chemistry needs. Even so, if you live in a hard water area, it is easier to set up an aquarium for fish that naturally occur in this environment, such as cichlids from the Rift Valley lakes of Africa. Conversely, having soft water means you can keep fish such as the discus (*Symphysodon* species) from the Amazonian region. However, by modifying the water chemistry in your tank (see pages 44–45), you can keep a wider variety of fish.

Although most fish for sale are small because they are young, aquarium fish vary significantly in size. Some catfish and cichlids, for example, can grow 12 inches (30cm) long and will become too big for your tank. Avoid overstocking the tank (see page 49).

Getting along together

Many fish such as tetras live in shoals. They are docile and you can keep them with nonaggressive fish that need similar water conditions, such as *Corydoras* catfish, creating a "community aquarium." Keep other fish with predatory natures, such as the red-tailed catfish (*Phractocephalus hemioliopterus*), on their own.

Aggressive behavior occurs among the same species. Males of the Siamese fighting fish (*Betta splendens*) will attack other species with similar colors such as red-tailed black sharks *(Epalzeorhynchus bicolor),* believing them to be rivals. Territorial disputes also arise at breeding time. Keeping odd numbers of fish, such as a group of five, creates greater harmony than pairs. Provide tank decor and plants to create hiding places for the fish.

Choose only healthy fish, such as this African cichlid. Once the fish are caught and are in plastic bags to go home, give them a final inspection. You'll be able to see more closely if they appear well.

What to look for

Many pet stores stock common varieties of fish, such as goldfish and guppies. You can find a wider selection of species at speciality aquatic centers. Check the fish before buying them, inspecting all of the fish in the tank as they swim around. Look for early signs of diseases (see pages 175–77).

Healthy fish are brightly colored, depending on the species, not pale. They swim easily through the water. Any fish that floats at an abnormal angle is probably ill. However, bear in mind that some fish will be reluctant to swim, especially catfish.

The body shape of the fish should be well-muscled, not shrunken toward the rear. This indicates an old fish or one with a chronic illness. Look for missing scales. Any damage to the body can lead to a fungal infection (see pages 174–75).

Check the fins. Elongated fins may be slightly ragged at their tips. Do not be concerned unless the area is severely frayed, with signs of fungus. Minor inflammation around the fin occurs when fish have been recently moved. Once they are in a permanent home, minor fin damage will heal.

must know

Good beginners' choices
▶ Goldfish
▶ Corydoras catfish
▶ Platy
▶ Neon tetra
▶ Dwarf gourami

Not for beginners
▶ Red-tailed black catfish *(Phractocephalus hemioliopterus):* grows large
▶ Honey gourami *(Colisa sota):* somewhat delicate
▶ Shark catfish *(Arius seemani):* predatory
▶ Jack Dempsey cichlid *(Cichlisoma octopasciatum):* aggressive
▶ Ocellated freshwater stingray *(Potamotrygon motoro):* dangerous

How fish work

With their ancestors first appearing in the world's oceans about 500 million years ago, fish represent the most numerous group of vertebrates, consisting of more than 27,000 different species. Today, fish display a huge diversity in shape and form.

Although a diverse group, fish still have a number of features in common. One of the most significant of these is their means of breathing. Fish rely on a pair of gills to allow them to extract oxygen from water. Water is drawn in through the mouth, flows over the gills, where oxygen enters the bloodstream and carbon dioxide diffuses into the water, which is then expelled from the body. The gill movements are often imperceptible, but if the fish is distressed or has difficulty in breathing, they are more pronounced.

Some fish that live in slow-flowing, stagnant, and poorly oxygenated waters have evolved auxiliary means of breathing. They gulp air directly from the

The gills on a fish are located on each side of the head, behind the eyes, and are protected by a flap called the operculum. Fish have a number of different fins to help them swim effectively in water.

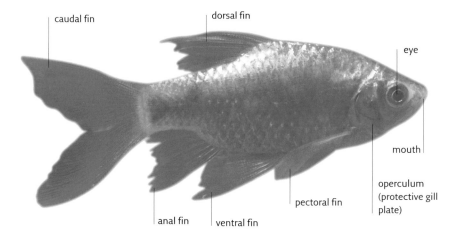

caudal fin

dorsal fin

eye

mouth

operculum (protective gill plate)

pectoral fin

anal fin

ventral fin

surface, which passes into their swim bladder. This organ usually allows the fish to adjust its position in the water. The anabantoids have evolved a different method of supplementary breathing, relying on special labyrinth organs located next to their gills.

External protection

Most fish have a body covering consisting of hard, overlapping scales to provide them with protection, but the size and shape of these scales vary. Some catfish, such as members of the *Corydoras* group, rely on bony plates instead of scales to protect their bodies. These are effective but restrict the fish's mobility. In contrast, more active catfish belonging to the *Synodontis* genus have sacrificed both scales and plates, relying on well-lubricated, thickened skin to defend themselves against both predators and infections of the body.

Where do they live ?

The appearance of most fish gives important clues about their lifestyle and the area of the tank they occupy. In bottom-feeding fish, such as loricariid catfish, the mouth is underneath the body. These fish are sluggish by nature, and their body shape allows them to lie on the base of the tank and hide.

Fish that are active by nature have a much more streamlined appearance, and they often have a deeply forked caudal fin, which allows them to power through the water with minimum effort. Those with upward-pointing jaws and a flat upper body profile, such as hatchetfish, live and feed close to the surface of the water. Fish that occupy the mid-water level, such as tetras, have jaws that are evenly balanced, combined with a streamlined, symmetrical body shape.

want to know more?

Take it to the next level...

▶ **The tank** 16–27
▶ **Fish profiles** 56–165
▶ **Keeping your fish healthy** 168–77

Other sources...

▶ **Specialized aquatic centers:** To purchase a wider range of fish and for advice on caring for them

▶ **Internet sources:** Do a search for the specific types of fish you want to keep for additional information

▶ **Aquatic societies:** Some hold regular meetings, providing a social dimension to fish keeping

2 The tank

Setting up an aquarium is generally a straightforward procedure, and you can achieve either a traditional or a more contemporary design without difficulty. You can choose from all-in-one units, incorporating everything you need, or buy the tank and the components separately. The most important thing is to decide where you want to position the tank before starting to equip it, because once it is full of water, it will be impossible to be moved without emptying it.

Choosing the tank

There are a number of choices that you'll have to make before setting up the aquarium, including deciding on the type of fish you want to keep, and these decisions will effect the type of tank you buy and the equipment it will need.

watch out!

Avoid being tempted by a tank in the shape of a vertical tower. A tower provides little horizontal swimming space for fish and has a small surface area compared with its volume of water. This results in a less efficient gaseous exchange—this takes place at the air-water interface, with carbon dioxide diffusing out of the water and being replaced by oxygen. The surface area of the aquarium is a significant factor in determining its stocking density (see pages 48-49).

The first decision is whether you want to keep coldwater fish such as goldfish, or tropical fish, which require a heated aquarium. The expense of running a heating system is low, and heaters that incorporate integral thermostats are inexpensive, so cost is not a consideration. In any case, you will still need a filtration system and a light over the tank, and both of these will require an electrical supply.

A coldwater tank may be more suitable for children if they are caring for the fish on their own, because there is no risk that they can accidentally burn themselves when servicing the tank. However, even this is not a problem if children want to keep tropical fish—external tank heaters with separate thermostats, which will prevent accidents, are available. An acrylic tank will be safer and lighter for a child to handle than a glass unit, although its sides can be easily scratched.

Decide where you want to place the aquarium in your home before buying it, so that you can select one that will fit in the chosen space, considering both its size and shape. It is often better to position the aquarium against a wall in the room where it will be out of direct sunlight, especially around the middle of the day, when the sun is usually at its hottest. However, brief morning sunlight can be

beneficial on occasions, especially to encourage spawning behavior in cyprinids and other species.

The rectangular tank is the most common type of aquarium. It provides a good surface area, compared to a smaller round bowl and tower tanks.

Aquarium designs

Glass tanks are made in a wide variety of shapes, such as the traditional rectangular design, bowl shape, and more unusual modern designs. Bear in mind that it may be difficult to find an undergravel filter plate to fit over the entire base, so you'll need an alternative filtration method. Triangular glass tanks are available to enliven the corner of a room. Most of these come with a cabinet, which also includes a hood for lighting purposes. Custom-made aquaria of this type are more expensive compared with those of a more conventional design.

A free-standing aquarium can be supported on a stand, instead of being incorporated into a cabinet, or it can be placed on a piece of furniture. Make sure that the furniture is sturdy enough for the weight of the tank when filled with water.

must know

You need to consider the following factors before buying an aquarium:
▶ Coldwater or tropical fish
▶ Where to position the tank (avoiding too much sunlight)
▶ Shape and size of the tank
▶ Free-standing or incorporated into a cabinet

weblinks: www.aqualink.com

Heating the tank

Keeping the water in your tank at the right temperature is important, and you may need a heater. However, not all fish require additional heating if they are kept at a typical room temperature, especially if you live in a hot region.

The aquarium heater usually fits inside the tank, where it must be fully submerged under water when switched on. Always allow it to cool before removing it from the tank. If you have a shallow aquarium—for killifish perhaps—use a short heater.

The output of heaters differs and is measured in watts. The heat output your tank needs depends on the volume of the tank. Look for a table on the back of the packaging to help you choose the correct heater for your tank. As a guide, there should be 1–2 watts per 1¼ gallons (0.2–0.5 watts per liter). This is not always consistent because a tank containing a large volume of water will hold its temperature more effectively than a small tank.

Most internal aquarium heaters also incorporate an integral thermostat, and this combined unit is known as a heaterstat. The thermostat regulates the heat output from the unit and is preset to about 75°F (24°C). You can raise the water temperature slightly to encourage spawning activity by turning a knob at the top of the unit. Otherwise, the preset temperature is suitable for a tropical aquarium.

The heaterstat fits at the back of the tank, where it can be disguised by the decor. There must be free circulation of water around the unit, so that colder water is brought into contact with the heater. The

unit is supplied
with a holder that
attaches to the side
of the aquarium.
Position it at an
angle to allow the
heated water to rise
and be circulated
by convection
currents and pull
cooler water into
contact with the

heater below. This provides a more consistent water
temperature and prevents the heated water from
contacting the thermostat and turning the unit off.

**Do not include fish that excavate
the ground for food, such as this
oscar (Astronotus ocellatus), or
that are large in a tank with a
heaterstat. For these fish, use
an external undertank heater.**

Undertank heating

An external heater, in the form of a thin pad that
lies under the base of the aquarium, is best for
large or destructive fish, but you'll need a separate
thermostat that fits within the tank to control the
pad. You should also use undertank heating in
breeding tanks if the water is shallow or if there is
a risk of eggs being deposited on the heater.

Temperature readings

An aquarium thermometer is essential to ensure
that the heating system is working effectively. You
can purchase the traditional internal, alcohol-filled
thermometer, but LCD designs, with a color strip
behind the temperature reading, are often preferred.
They fit on the outside of the aquarium and are
easier to read, but you need to attach them properly
onto the tank to provide an accurate reading.
Position the thermometer at the farthest point
away from the heater, where the water is coldest.

Lights and lighting

Lighting in a fish tank can enhance your tank setup, illuminate your fish, and help keep your plants healthy. Special fluorescent lights will bring out the color in red fish, while night lights will highlight twilight feeders, such as catfish.

watch out!

It is extremely important that the electrical attachments for the lights are properly screened, so they cannot be splashed accidentally and are not exposed to condensation. The coverings at the ends of the lights must be waterproof—rubber caps are available for this purpose.

The lighting positioned above an aquarium is not only essential to allow you to see the fish clearly—especially when looking for signs of a disease or for indications that a pair of fish are ready to spawn—but it is also vital for healthy aquatic plants. The plants living in your tank rely on light as a source of energy, which allows them to undertake the process known as photosynthesis. When photosynthesizing, the plants use the carbon dioxide discharged by the fish and release oxygen into the water—this will help contribute to the well-being of the fish.

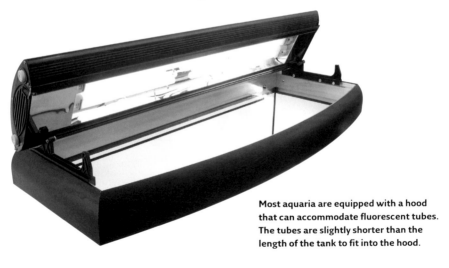

Most aquaria are equipped with a hood that can accommodate fluorescent tubes. The tubes are slightly shorter than the length of the tank to fit into the hood.

Not all lights are suitable for an aquarium. Plants need to be exposed to specific wavelengths of light to be able to photosynthesize. You should use special fluorescent lights that mimic the effects of sunlight. They have the additional benefit of emitting light rather than heat, so they will not affect the water temperature – unlike ordinary tungsten bulbs. You'll need at least one full spectrum tube for photosynthesis.

The output of lighting varies, and more powerful lighting is necessary above deeper aquaria. There should be a minimum of 4 watts of light for each 1¼ gallons (4.5 liters) of water.

The output from fluorescent lights declines progressively, so it is usually recommended to replace them every nine months or so, even if they are still working. This will ensure that the plant growth remains healthy. When buying replacement fluorescent light tubes, make sure you remember to take note of the size of your tank. The tubes are available in various lengths, and you'll need to purchase the correct size for your tank.

Special lighting

In some cases, it can be advantageous to run two tubes in parallel. This will allow you to incorporate one tube to highlight the coloration of the fish, especially those that are red, along with a full spectrum tube.

You could also incorporate a special night light. This provides a low level of illumination, allowing the movements of cave-dwelling fish that live in dark surroundings to be observed clearly. This lighting also can be useful when keeping various catfish and other species that naturally become more active from dusk onward.

must know

The length of time that the lights are left on is important. If they are switched on for only a short time each day, there will not be sufficient light for plant growth. However, excessive light exposure can lead to excessive algal growth, which is not only unsightly but can also result in the dying back of plants if they are covered with it. On average, the aquarium lighting should be left on for 10 to 12 hours per day. You can control the lighting with a switch on a timer if necessary.

Gravel and rockwork

Gravel provides an attractive base for your tank, but depending on your choice it either drains or enhances the colour of the fish. Rockwork can create an interesting focal point—and it gives fish that have a timid nature a convenient place to hide.

The covering used on the base of the aquarium is important if an undergravel filtration system is fitted, because the gravel must be coarse enough to allow water to flow through its irregular shapes. There are various types of aquarium gravel available, some of which are brightly colored. These rarely work as well as natural stones because of the optical effect they create, with bright red gravel draining the color of red fish, such as some swordtails (see pages 130-31) and goldfish (see pages 138-41). White gravel can result in the fish appearing paler than normal and cause them to react in the same way as if they were under bright lights.

Natural gravel creates a neutral background for plants and won't distract from the colors of bright fish. Dark substrates work more effectively than light ones.

Gravel comprising of natural stones creates a neutral background. When assessing the quantity of

gravel required, allow approximately 2 pounds (1kg) per gallon (3.75 liters), based on the tank's volume.

Rockwork

Rockwork helps to create a natural backdrop and provides retreats for the fish. It can also look attractive—remember that its natural coloration appears brighter when it is wet. You can purchase various types of stone for an aquarium from an aquatic store, and these are usually sold on the basis of their weight. It helps if you have a plan for your aquarium before purchasing the rocks so you have an idea of where they will fit. Try not to cover too much of the base of the aquarium with rockwork, because this can affect the efficiency of an undergravel filter.

As an alternative to natural rockwork, you can obtain artificial lightweight rockwork designed for use in aquaria. These are available at aquatic stores.

The type of rockwork you choose will be influenced by the type of fish that you are keeping. Limestone rocks are unsuitable for aquaria where soft, acidic water conditions are required. Various fish, including a number of cichlids, spawn on rockwork. For this purpose, you should include an inert rock, such as slate, in their aquarium.

Rockwork is heavy and needs to be securely positioned in the aquarium to prevent it from falling over. This is most likely to occur in tanks accommodating active fish, such as Central American cichlids, many of which dig in the substrate. For fish that spawn in caves, a better option is to place a clean section of a clay flowerpot on the floor of the tank instead of trying to create a cave from loose rocks that can collapse.

must know

Aquarium gravel may not be an inert substance and can have a marked effect on the chemistry of the water in the tank. Using calcareous gravel reinforces the hard, alkaline water conditions that Rift Valley cichlids require in their aquarium, but do not use it for fish such as discus (see pages 100–1), which need soft, acidic water. The same applies in the case of rockwork.

Filters and what they do

Filters are necessary to maintain a healthy environment in the aquarium. There is a choice of undergravel filters, power filters, and external filters. They help to break down the fishes' waste and assist oxygenation of the water.

Fish in an aquarium live in higher densities than they do in the wild. There is no flow of water to flush through their waste, which accumulates in their surroundings and threatens their health. Filtration helps to remove the harmful ammonia produced by the fish, so is essential in maintaining a healthy environment. It saves the need to empty the tank on a regular basis, which is distressing for the fish.

Waste breakdown

The ammonia from the fish and the decomposition of other waste matter, such as any uneaten food, is detoxified by a series of chemical reactions from beneficial bacteria in the tank. This forms part of the nitrogen cycle, with the ammonia being broken down to nitrite and then to nitrate, which can be used by plants as a fertilizer. This is the result of biological filtration.

In a new aquarium, there is not a viable population of these bacteria to undertake this conversion. You'll need to seed a biological filter with a culture of beneficial bacteria, which can then multiply in the aquarium. You can add zeolite

An undergravel filter system consists of a plate that fits over the entire base of the aquarium, with the gravel on top acting as a filter bed where the bacterial population develops.

to remove ammonia before the biological system is fully effective, which may take up to two months.

Types of filtration

An undergravel filter is a simple type of biological filter. There must be a good water flow through the gravel above it so that there is enough oxygen for the bacteria to thrive. A coarse gravel is needed for this purpose at a depth of 2 inches (5cm) above the filter plate. An air pump is also necessary. It should have a non-return valve to eliminate the risk of water running back into the pump, and it must never be covered because this presents a fire risk.

Many tanks have a power filter consisting of an integral pump and a foam core. It relies on both biological and mechanical filtration. Position it with the outflow just at the surface to increase oxygenation in the water by creating a current.

Bigger tanks will benefit from an external filter, which can be hidden in a cabinet. It draws water out of the tank and passes it through a filtration system, which may include activated carbon. This carries out chemical filtration, binding chemicals extracted from the water. This type of filtration is not suitable for aquaria where fish are treated with medication.

There is a range of more complex filters on the market. Trickle filters, for example, draw water from the tank and oxygenate it as it runs down through the filter. Other media may also be used.

To monitor the effectiveness of the filtration system, carry out regular water tests (see page 44–45). These will alert you to problems that can endanger the fish.

want to know more?

Take it to the next level...

▶ **Plants** 28–37
▶ **Setting up and maintaining your tank** 38–55

Other sources...
▶ **Specialized aquatic centers: For equipment**

▶ **Internet sources: For most recent information about aquarium equipment**

▶ **Fish-keeping magazines: To keep up to date about keeping fish**

▶ **Aquatic societies: For on-going advice on fish keeping**

▶ **Manufacturers' leaflets: To learn about the equipment you purchase**

Beneficial bacteria populate the foam core, which has several layers of foam. The foam core also traps larger particles of waste.

3 Plants

Aquatic plants provide a natural backdrop for the fish in the aquarium, and they also fulfill a number of important roles. They offer vital cover, especially at breeding time, and utilize the waste produced by the fish, creating a better environment. Live plants can also provide a source of food for some fish. However, live plants may not thrive under all conditions, so sometimes lifelike plastic aquarium plants may be preferable.

Aquatic plants and snails

Both living aquatic plants and plastic plants have their place in the aquarium, adding to its appearance and creating useful hiding places. Ornamental snails are sometimes housed in a tank, although they are often considered invasive.

Some plants, such as Canadian pondweed *(Elodea canadensis)*, are a supplement to the diet of certain fish, including the zebra danio *(Brachydanio rerio)*. These fish also like to spawn in plants.

Realistic-looking plastic plants do not detract from the overall appearance of the aquarium, and they are easy to incorporate in the design of the tank. Plastic plants are often supplied with a weighted base, which you can simply bury under the substrate, or you can weigh it down by other tank decor if the fish like to excavate the substrate.

Incorporating living plants into the aquarium requires time and patience, but they create a more natural environment and improve water conditions for the fish. Choose the plants carefully to ensure they will not outgrow the tank. Curtail their growth by keeping them in small pots to ensure that their roots do not spread too far through the substrate. If allowed to spread, the roots can block the holes in an undergravel filter, reducing its efficiency.

Some fish with a timid nature, such as many of the tetras, will feel more at ease in an aquarium that includes plenty of plants in which they can hide.

The way in which living aquatic plants are treated will have an impact on the ease in which they can be established in new surroundings. You should always handle them carefully, and never allow their leaves to dry out at any stage. When you purchase new plants, submerge them in water of the correct temperature at the earliest opportunity.

It is not uncommon for some dieback of the leaves to occur after moving a plant, particularly in the case of more delicate species. However, as long as the environmental conditions are suitable, new growth should soon appear. The lighting in the aquarium (see pages 22–23) is important at this stage, and it may help to use a special aquatic plant fertilizer until the plant becomes established.

You can use plastic and living plants in the same tank, as here with red ludwigia (*Ludwigia repens*). Take out the plastic ones once the real plants spread.

Snails

Aquatic snails are easily introduced to an aquarium by accident as eggs on the leaves of plants. The egg masses are transparent and jellylike in appearance. While a few snails add a focus of interest in the tank and their scavenging feeding habits may help to clear up uneaten food, they often breed so readily that their numbers can become overwhelming, resulting in the destruction of the aquatic plants on which they feed. It is hard to curtail the breeding habits of snails because they are "hermaphrodite"— they have both male and female sex organs present in their bodies. Keeping only two snails together will result in the production of fertile eggs.

The best way to control aquatic snails is to remove egg deposits from the tank before they have the chance to hatch. There are some aquarium fish, such as pufferfish (see page 165), that will prey upon snails, and they may even eliminate them from an aquarium.

Certain aquatic snails, including the ornamental golden form of the apple snail (*Pomacea bridgesi*), require warmer water conditions than others because they are from tropical parts of the world.

Creating a planting scheme

To work effectively, the plants in an aquarium should merge alongside other decor, such as rockwork and bogwood. It is also important to consider the habits of the fish, using the plants to complement their natural behavior.

You can use a planting stick to position a plant in an established tank. Tools are available at aquatic stores to help you plant and maintain aquatic plants.

In a community aquarium with a variety of fish, you'll need plants in different parts of the tank. If you include surface feeders among your fish, then provide floating plants, which they can hide below. Within the main body of water, place plants in several areas, which again can be used as hiding places, but at the same time make sure you leave an open area where they have plenty of room to swim.

The needs of the fish are important, but also consider the appearance of the plants in the tank. Establish the likely height to which the plants will grow. If you want to emphasize the width of the aquarium, position smaller plants in the foreground and around the sides of the tank, and allow them to merge with larger plants toward the back. This arrangement will also make it easier for you to watch the fish. You can also add a single, more striking specimen plant in the central area, toward the back of the tank.

Some degree of trial-and-error will be necessary as you blend the plants alongside other aquarium decor. You should start with a selection of plants that will not outgrow the size of your tank. Be careful not to plant the aquarium too heavily in the beginning and allow for the growth of the plants, just as if you were planting a flower border.

Bogwood

Pieces of bogwood, an important planting medium in the aquarium, are available from aquatic stores. This type of wood has been submerged in a boggy area for a long period, and during the time it becomes full of tannin, which will turn the aquarium water yellowish. Before adding bogwood to your tank you should soak it in water, changing the water regularly until it stays clear.

Floating plants are important to fish that live close to the surface such as hatchetfish (*Carnegiella strigata*), providing them with cover where they can feel secure.

You can attach plants, such as Java moss (*Vesicularia dubyana*), to the bogwood with a rubber band until it anchors itself in due course. The bogwood will provide cover under which various bottom-feeders will retreat. Once established, its thick growth will provide important retreats for the young fry of live-bearers such as guppies (see pages 126–27). Another plant that will grow well on bogwood is Java fern (*Microsorium pteropus*).

(see pages 126–27)

must know

When planning a planting scheme, be sure to determine the specific species of plant that you are buying. For example, *Cryptocoryne nevillii* can grow 3 inches (7.5cm) tall, while the leaves on *C. ciliata* may reach up to 24 inches (60cm) long.

Aquatic plants established alongside bogwood make a perfect retreat for bottom-feeders and live-bearers alike.

A directory of aquatic plants

Aquatic plants can be divided into two categories: those that are anchored in the substrate and those that float on the water surface. Substrate plants can be subdivided into tall background and space fillers, low-level plants, and specimen plants.

Before buying aquatic plants you should examine their condition. Healthy plants are well colored, appearing green instead of yellow. They may be sold as sprigs, which will root easily in the substrate, or as rooted plants, sometimes displaying offsets. You can purchase some in a dormant form, such as bulbs, which simply need to be potted up. Aquatic plants do not usually require a soil-based growing medium, but if you pot them up, you'll need to use a special aquatic soil for this purpose. It is available from aquatic stores specializing in ponds, as well as from some garden centers.

You can use specimen plants, such as this swordplant *(Echinodorus species)*, to make an attractive highlight in the tank. Its bright green leaves will be a perfect foil to colorful fish.

Floating plants

Plants that float along the surface of the water have long roots that dangle in the water, and they are wafted around by the surface currents. These plants are often fast growers and require regular pruning. They make excellent retreats for young fry as well as surface-feeders. Make sure you include them in a breeding tank for bubble-nest builders.

Substrate plants

Aquatic plants that grow in or close to the base of the aquarium are known as substrate plants. They vary significantly in size, and also in terms of the growing conditions that they require. Although these plants are decorative, they are also functional, providing fish a place to hide or lay eggs.

You can let Canadian pondweed (*Elodea canadensis*) **float or weigh it down in the substrate.**

Plants for different fish

Although these plants are suitable for many fish, they are especially beneficial in certain situations:
▶ Vallisneria is ideal for angelfish (*Pterophyllum* species, see pages 104–5) because its tall, reedlike shape enables the tall, narrow-bodied fish to weave between the fronds.
▶ Fairy moss *(Azolla caroliniana)* suits bubble-nest builders, such as Siamese fighting fish (*Betta splendens*)—it offers anchor points for their nests.
▶ Tropical hornwort *(Ceratophyllum submersum)* can be useful as a spawning plant, catching and retaining the eggs as they drift downwards.
▶ Amazon swordplants *(Echinodorus* species) are ideal for an aquarium housing fish that may destroy aquatic vegetation—these plants are tough and grow quickly.
▶ Java moss *(Vesicularia dubyana)* can create an attractive covering on rockwork and bogwood, as well as provide an ideal retreat for young fry.
▶ Mangrove species will thrive in a brackish water aquarium, growing partly out of the water.

The straplike leaves of vallisneria may be curled, as in the case of the twisted vallisneria (*Vallisneria tortifolia*).

Floating plants

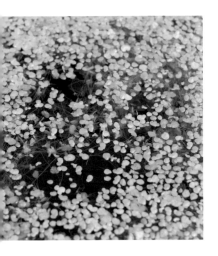

Duckweed can form a dense mat and thrives under brightly lit conditions. It is often found in coldwater tanks, but you can grow it in a tropical setup, too.

▶ **Duckweed** (*Lemna* species) is a small plant that grows readily over the surface of the aquarium. Add a few pieces to the tank and it will multiply rapidly. Duckweed provides food for some vegetarian fish.

▶ **Fairy moss** (*Azolla caroliniana*) is adaptable to many water temperatures, but it prefers hard water conditions. Bright illumination is important to encourage its growth. Young fry often cluster between its dark roots. Fairy moss is an ideal choice in an aquarium where diffused lighting is needed.

▶ **Water lettuce** (*Pistia stratiotes*), or Nile cabbage, is so-called because of its appearance, because it looks like a floating vegetable. It requires a heated tank with a sufficient gap between the water surface and the hood to allow ventilation, which prevents the plants from damping off and rotting.

▶ **Indian fern** (*Ceratopteris thalictroides*) is an unusual plant in that it grows well if planted in the substrate, yet it can also grow just as easily as a floating plant at the water's surface. Old plants produce buds that float up to the surface, where they develop. It is an ideal choice for an Amazonian tank with soft and acidic water conditions.

▶ **Crystalwort** (*Riccia fluitans*) does not grow on the surface of the water but is usually found just below it, forming dense clumps. It provides good protection for young live-bearers, helping them to remain out of reach of the adults. It grows rapidly, by vegetative division, so just break off pieces from an existing plant to create new growth.

must know

When choosing plants for the aquarium, it is important to consider not only their size, but also other factors that influence their growth such as the water and lighting conditions in the tank.

Substrate plants

▶ **Cryptocorynes** are a versatile group, with up to 30 varieties available for tropical aquaria. They are adaptable in their water chemistry needs, and some thrive in brackish water conditions. Cryptocorynes are often sold as cuttings. Some need more brightly lit surroundings than others. Check on the growth of individual species—some can become tall.

▶ **Sagittarias**, a diverse group, thrive in heated water. They spread by runners, forming dense stands of growth. Some species grow taller than others. The dwarf sagittaria reaches 6 inches (15cm) in height, making it ideal for the sides of the tank.

▶ **Vallisneria,** or tape grass, have straplike leaves. They are valued for their adaptable growing habits, but they tend to grow better in a heated aquarium.

▶ **Canadian pondweed** (*Elodea canadensis*) is popular in coldwater tanks. It is a good choice in a tank with goldfish, which often dig in the substrate. If pieces start to become leggy, cut off and retain the top 3 inches (7.5cm)—the shoots will grow rapidly.

▶ **False tenellus** (*Lilaeopsis brasiliensis*) grows to only 3 inches (7.5cm) high, so it is ideal for the front of a tank. The strands create a grasslike area. It adapts to lighting, but does not thrive at high temperatures.

▶ **Variegated hygrophilia** (*Hygrophilia* species) displays reddish and purple hues, complementing both green plants around them and the color of the fish. Variegated hygrophilia is ideal for a tropical tank, growing well in a range of water conditions.

want to know more?

Take it to the next level...

▶ **Setting up and maintaining your tank** 38-55
▶ **Breeding** 178-185

Other sources...

▶ **Specialized aquatic centers: To purchase a wider selection of plants for your tank**

▶ **Internet sources: Do a search for specific plants for additional information**

▶ **Aquatic societies: For advice on caring for more specialized plants**

▶ **Other publications: Once you're ready to consider adding specialized plants to your tank**

4 Setting up and maintaining your tank

Setting up an aquarium is usually a simple procedure, but check that everything is functioning properly before acquiring the fish. Otherwise, if something does go wrong, such as the heater failing, the fish will be stranded in their transport bags until you can resolve the problem. Maintenance is also straightforward, but it can be more time-consuming until the filtration system is fully operational.

Tank setup

Setting up a tank is straightforward as long as you proceed in a practical order. The first stage is to position the aquarium, because once you add the gravel and water, you won't be able to move it again without emptying the tank.

watch out!

▶ Do not place any ordinary household objects in the aquarium, because these may be toxic to the fish.

Start by rinsing out your aquarium in case the interior is dusty or there are any small spicules of glass from the manufacturing process. Then put the tank in position on its base, which must be level to lessen the water pressure on the joints at the corners of the tank. Check the levelness by using a level. If the floor of the room slopes, you can adjust the position of the furniture or stand by using wooden blocks to ensure the tank is correctly leveled.

If you have an all-glass aquarium, place it on a sheet of polystyrene plastic, which will absorb any minor unevenness in the surface of the base. If you are using an undertank heater, sandwich it between the plastic and the tank so that it is in direct contact with the underside of the aquarium.

Adding a backdrop

If you want to use a backdrop, carefully secure it in place. This will conceal anything behind the aquarium such as a patterned wallpaper, which may otherwise spoil the natural appearance of the tank. It is usually better to choose a relatively neutral backdrop that extends the aquarium, instead of one that has a nonaquatic theme, which could distract from it. Backdrops are available in various designs and sizes to fit aquaria of different sizes.

▶ The filter

If you are using an undergravel filter, place the filter plate inside the tank directly onto the base. Make sure the uplift tube is fitted along with the airline, which will ultimately be connected to the air pump.

◀ The gravel

Before placing the gravel in the tank—even if it is labeled as pre-washed—rinse it thoroughly in a colander until the water runs clear. If you don't rinse it, the water will become cloudy in the tank. Once the gravel is clean, tip it gently into the tank, then create a slight slope running from the back of the tank to the front. This will help you to find uneaten food that may otherwise rot out of sight.

▶ The tank decor

Put in any tank decor, such as rockwork, but first scrub it with a clean brush to remove any dirt. Position the rockwork firmly in the tank, burying it slightly into the gravel to prevent dirt accumulating around it. Allow sufficient space to put plants in at a later stage, as well as bogwood. You can add various decorative items, such as airstones, which create bubbles to help circulate the water.

The various electrical equipment, such as the filter, heaterstat, and lights, will require connecting a number of plugs to the electrical supply. You should avoid using adaptors in electrical outlets to take a larger number of plugs because this is potentially unsafe. It is safer to run the plugs to a single electrical outlet via a safe multi-plug extension cable, which can be hidden out of sight.

The heaterstat and power filter

Put the heaterstat in place, but do not connect it to the power supply. The same applies if you are using a power filter with the undergravel filter or on its own. Position the power filter by one of the side panels, with the output nozzle directed along the length of the tank to create a good current. Avoid positioning it with a rock or similar obstruction in front, which may affect the inlet to the filter. Place the thermometer inside the aquarium or on the glass at the front—keep it away from the heaterstat.

▼ Filling the tank

Place a clean container or a saucer on the gravel. Using a clean watering can reserved for adding water to the tank, pour the water onto it to minimize disturbance to the base. Use neutralized water from the cold-water faucet instead of mixing it with hot tap water. This will ensure that the heaterstat is working effectively—switch it on once you have filled the tank with water, and allow it to heat the water. You can monitor its effectiveness with the thermometer. (Never switch the heaterstat on out of the water—this is dangerous). Do not forget to add the beneficial bacterial culture. It will help to seed the filter bed and is essential before you can add the fish to the tank.

▶ Adding the plants

Once the water temperature has stabilized, after about a day, set the plants in place, following your planting scheme. Position them by hand, or use a planting tool if the plants are not in pots to avoid disturbing the surrounding area. For floating plants, allow them to drift over the surface.

cover glass

You can fit a combination of types of lighting in the hood

Place the thermometer where it will be easy to read but away from the heaterstat

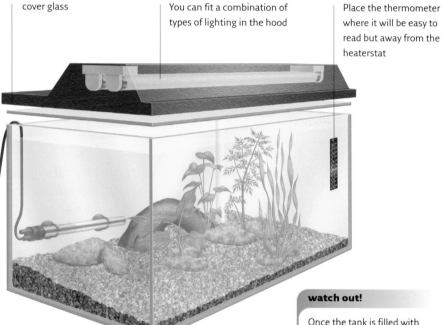

▲ The finished tank

Connect the lights and make sure that they are working properly. Over the next day or two, monitor the water temperature to make sure the heaterstat is also working. If it is, then your aquarium is ready for some fish (see pages 48–51).

watch out!

Once the tank is filled with water, it is vital to always turn off the electrical equipment before you place your hand in it, particularly in case there is an accident. For example, if you dislodge a rockwork and smash the heaterstat, you can receive a severe or even fatal shock.

Water

Aquarium fish are naturally found in a range of different water conditions around the world. All water has the same chemical formula of H2O, but it can differ significantly in its relative hardness and acidity, which is measured on the pH scale.

watch out!

Tap water contains chlorine or chloramine, which makes it safe for drinking. Unfortunately, both these chemicals are toxic to fish. It is essential to neutralize them by using a water conditioner that contains a dechlorinator. Always remember to treat new water, not just when setting up the tank, but also whenever doing partial water changes.

When rain falls the water is relatively pure and free from mineral salts. The chemical constitution of rainwater changes when it comes into contact with the ground, especially in a limestone area. This mineral is soluble in water, and by running over and through limestone rocks, calcium salts dissolve in the rainwater, affecting its chemistry. This causes what is typically described as "hard water," which is evident at home when you wash your hands with soap. If you live in a hard-water area, the tap water will not form a lather readily due to the presence of calcium salts. Fresh rainwater or water that has not run through limestone is described as "soft," and it will create a lather rapidly.

It is possible to separate some calcium salts, such as calcium bicarbonate, from hard water by boiling the water. This is what happens in hard-water areas when kettles fur up because of calcium deposits. This is known as temporary hardness, and it is often abbreviated "KH" (originally from the German *karbonate)*. Conversely, permanent hardness cannot be affected by boiling, because it is caused by different types of salts, such as calcium sulfate. There are a number of different ways of measuring the relative hardness of water, and test kits are available from aquatic stores.

It is possible to alter the chemical composition of tap water due to a process known as reverse osmosis (abbreviated as "RO"). This entails using a membrane to extract the dissolved chemicals to create softer water. To make the water harder, add limestone to the tank.

pH and its significance

In water chemistry, the pH reflects its hydrogen ion concentration. This is linked to the hardness of the water—soft water is acidic while hard water is alkaline. Fish that originate from hard-water areas will prefer alkaline conditions, and those from a soft-water area prefer acidic water. The water pH is measured on a log-based scale running from pH 0, the extreme acidic side of the scale, up to pH 14, which is the most alkaline reading; pH 7.0 is neutral. Because pH is measured on a log-based scale, a small shift of only one unit reflects a tenfold increase in the hydrogen ion concentration in the water. A change of one unit can have serious consequences for the fish.

Changes within the tank, resulting from the breakdown of waste as part of the nitrogen cycle, can impact directly on the pH. It will fall as the level of dissolved pollutants increases, and the stabilizing effects of the water—which is known as its "buffering capacity"—are used up. The pH shifts are more potentially dangerous in tanks where the water is alkaline, because there are fewer free hydrogen ions to combine with the ammonia.

To raise the pH in a tank, add limestone rockwork or gravel. To create more acidic surroundings, add aquarium peat to the tank—it may come in a sachet or you might need to add it to the filter. In the case of tetras, use a black-water extract to add tannin, which helps to acidify the water.

must know

The risk of problems in a new tank is greater in hard-water areas. Make sure you measure the pH in the water on a regular basis by using test kits or an LCD meter dipped in a water sample.

Special water conditions

Most commercially bred aquarium fish can adapt to changes in water conditions, but some fish are more sensitive to water chemistry than others. The amount of salt in the water can also make a difference to certain fish.

must know

You should check the salinity in the tank every week by using an instrument known as an hydrometer. Alternatively, you can use a conductivity meter, which will give a figure for the specific gravity of the water, known as the SG figure. In a brackish aquarium, this should be between 1.002 and 1.007.

Many gobies come from marine environments but the bumblebee goby (Hypogymnogobius xan-thozana) prefers brackish water.

The vast majority of freshwater aquarium fish are bred commercially on special farms around the world in centers ranging from Florida to Singapore. These farms are usually far away from their natural habitat, so the fish have often had to adapt to their surroundings and are far less sensitive to the water chemistry than their wild relatives.

Nevertheless, there are exceptions. For example, the discus (see pages 100–1) is sensitive to water chemistry. Other fish, such as many of the barbs, will thrive in hard-water conditions; however, they are more likely to spawn successfully in soft, acidic water, like their wild relatives. If the water conditions are not optimal, the fish will probably lose some of their coloration and appear duller than usual.

Water salinity and brackish aquaria

In some cases, the salinity of the water is important, especially for fish that originate from brackish water conditions. Creating suitable water conditions in an aquarium for these fish is straightforward, due to the availability of marine salt, which is specially formulated for this purpose. Make sure you follow the package instructions carefully because they differ slightly between brands.

The amount of salt required to create brackish water conditions is less than will be necessary for a marine tank, where the salt concentration in the water is higher. To add the salt, measure it out and dissolve it in the appropriate volume of water, stirring it with a wooden spoon. It may be necessary to make it in batches. The actual volume of water required is the total volume of the tank, which can be found by multiplying the length, width, and height together in centimeters and dividing by 1,000 for a figure in liters; divide this figure by 3.785 for gallons. As a guide, subtract ten percent from this total to allow for the tank decor and equipment— this is the functional volume of the tank.

Fish originating from estuaries, such as the green pufferfish (*Tetraodon fluviatilis*), often require brackish water.

Maintaining brackish water
Once the tank is established, avoid switching between salt brands when carrying out partial water changes. If the water level falls because of evaporation, it is important to top up the tank with only fresh water, treated as always with a dechlorinator. This is because it is the water that has evaporated, not the salt. If you add a fresh salt solution in these circumstances, you will increase the overall salinity within the aquarium.

must know

Fish for hard-water conditions
▶ Rift Valley cichlids
▶ Swordtails
▶ Mollies
▶ Platies
▶ Halfbeaks

Fish for soft-water conditions
▶ Discus
▶ Angelfish
▶ Tetras
▶ Annual killifish
▶ Loaches

Fish for brackish water
▶ Bumblebee goby
▶ Green pufferfish
▶ Indian glassfish
▶ Mollies

Adding fish to the tank

You can encourage aquarium fish to settle into their new home by helping them adjust gradually to their new water conditions and surroundings. The first few days are the most important because extra stress can make them vulnerable to disease.

Before purchasing your fish, make sure everything is working correctly in your tank setup and wait a day or two to make sure the heaterstat is functioning properly. You may not want to buy all the fish for the tank at the beginning, because the filtration system will not be working at maximum efficiency. Add about 50 percent of your total stocking density at first, then wait another six weeks before adding more fish. This will allow the bacteria developing in the filtration system, which feed on fish waste, to become fully established.

However, if you add other fish later on, they may be harried by the established tank occupants. You can try introducing the new arrivals at feeding time when the other fish will be distracted, or with the lights off. You will risk introducing illness to the established fish, especially if you do not quarantine the new fish for two weeks in another tank. It is less disruptive to introduce all the fish at once, but you'll need to monitor the water chemistry closely and carry out more frequent partial water changes.

Before making your purchase, inspect the fish after they have been caught and bagged. The bag may be left floating in the store's aquarium while you finish your transaction.

Purchasing the fish

Fish are often sold in plastic bags in a small volume of water compared with the enclosed oxygen, allowing the fish to be transported safely home. Do not delay your journey and travel with the fish carefully. Never leave them in the back of a car, for example, in direct sunlight. Keep the bag upright, and ensure that it cannot roll around to minimize the stress on the fish. You can wrap the plastic bag inside newspaper to create a dark environment for them or to provide insulation in cold weather.

Preparing to release the fish

When you arrive home, float the plastic bag at the surface of the aquarium for 20 minutes. This allows the temperature of the water in the bag to warm up gradually, so that when you release the fish the temperatures in the bag and tank will be similar. You may not need to do this for coldwater fish because the temperature difference may be less significant.

Before you add new arrivals to an aquarium, float the plastic bag in the tank until the water temperatures are the same. This will place less stress on the fish, although it is less necessary for coldwater fish.

must know

As a general guide to stocking capacity, allow approximately 1 gallon per 1 inch (1.5–2 liters of water per cm of fish). It is important not to stock the tank to its maximum capacity when first setting up a tank because the fish will need space to grow. You can use the figures in the Fish profiles section to determine a fish's adult size. The formula is only a guide.

Releasing the fish

The safest method for adding the fish to the tank is to use a net. Nets of various sizes are available for aquarium fish. The easiest way to transfer a fish is to pour the water carefully out of the bag through the net into a bucket. Place one hand over the top of the net while the fish is inside it, so that there is no risk of the fish jumping out as you move it into the aquarium. Lower the net, then turn it to one side and wait for the fish to swim out.

Don't be surprised if the fish are shy at first and hide among the plants or behind rockwork. Leave the aquarium lights off for a few hours to allow the fish to become familiar with their new surroundings.

By using a net to release the fish into your aquarium, you will avoid the possibility of adding contaminated water.

After a few hours offer them a little food—they won't eat much.

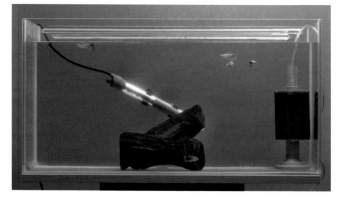

Keep a check on the fish for the first few days to ensure they settle in and remain healthy. Avoid overfeeding the fish because uneaten food will pollute the water and endanger their health. At feeding time observe the fish at closer quarters and see if they are eating well.

If you notice signs of illness in any of the fish, remove them from the tank without delay to safeguard the other occupants. Some fish keepers have a second quarantine tank for sick fish.

Partial water changes

Invest in a gravel cleaner to keep the substrate clean and do partial water changes. These are important in a new tank setup, as they prevent the build-up of dangerous nitrogenous waste in the water, which can threaten the health of the fish. Change about one-third of the water each week until the filtration system is working effectively. Add new water that is the same temperature as that within the tank, making sure that you first treat it with a water conditioner to neutralize chlorine or chloramine. You can use hot tap water to adjust the water temperature. Use a thermometer to make sure the temperature is the same as the water in the tank.

The influx of fresh water dilutes the waste in the tank, making it safer for the fish, and helps to lessen the burden on the filtration system while it is not functioning at maximum efficiency. Adding the compound zeolite in a sachet also helps, because it binds ammonia. Daily water tests in a new aquarium is the best way of determining the state of the water.

must know

While there may only be a small volume of water present within the plastic transport bags, it is not a good idea to tip it straight into the aquarium with the fish, because there can be potentially harmful microbes, such as fungal spores, present. Although these may not normally cause disease, they can multiply within a new tank, representing a potential hazard. It is often better to net the fish instead of tipping them with the water into the tank.

Ongoing maintenance

Even when the aquarium is well established, it will still need partial water changes, although less frequently. You'll also need to clean the gravel and foam filters and to prune the plants. By performing these tasks regularly, you'll keep your fish healthy.

> **must know**
>
> Whenever servicing the aquarium, it is a good idea to wear a pair of rubber gloves. This safeguards the fish from any potentially harmful chemical deposits on your hands, and it also ensures that you do not contract any illnesses present in the water if you have cuts on your hands.

For a well-established aquarium, carry out partial water changes about once every three weeks, depending on the water test results. Cleaning the gravel is also important, because mulm—a brownish accumulation of fish waste—can be drawn down between the stones, making the undergravel filter work less effectively. The gravel can be cleaned easily with a gravel cleaner, a plastic attachment on the siphon tube used to draw water out of the tank.

Using a gravel cleaner
Start by placing a bucket on the floor, below the level of the tank. Fill the tube of the gravel cleaner with dechlorinated water, and place your thumb over the bottom end to prevent the water from running into the bucket. Lower the gravel cleaner attachment over the gravel before releasing your thumb from the lower end. Water will flow freely out of the tank, with the gravel being stirred up in the cleaner. When the bucket is almost full, place your finger over the end of the tube and lift it up to break the flow.

Foam-filter maintenance
If you have a power filter, do not discard the old tank water from cleaning the gravel. Instead, dismantle the filter to remove its foam, which can also be

blocked by mulm. Do not clean it under a tap, because the chlorine or chloramine present can kill the beneficial bacteria in the foam. Squeeze the foam out in the bucket of old tank water to remove the mulm. Because of its nitrogen content, the water can be used for watering plants.

You may need to replace this sponge, but a new sponge will be devoid of bacteria, and this will reduce the effective level of filtration in the aquarium. Reseed the filter with a bacterial culture. This applies in the case of similar media in canister filters as well.

Until bacteria are established, the water may have a buildup of nitrogenous waste. Some fish are more tolerant than others, notably those that originate in slow-flowing stretches of water or ponds, compared with those found in turbulent waters, where the flow prevents the buildup of chemicals. The major danger period is usually after about a week, when the ammonia level is at its peak. It should decline, with nitrite levels increasing and reaching their maximum after a month. The nitrate levels will then rise, indicating that the filtration system is becoming mature.

Do not overload the filtration system during this crucial period. You can do this by overfeeding the fish, with the wasted food decomposing in the tank. A major surge in ammonia can also be triggered by the unnoticed death of a fish. For this reason, overstocking the aquarium can also be dangerous.

When using a gravel cleaner, the flow will not be strong enough to suck the gravel up into the tube and out of the tank. Move the cleaner over the gravel base, taking care not to uproot any plants and avoiding curious fish.

Aquarium lighting

It can be difficult to establish the correct level of lighting in a new aquarium. If it is too low, the plants will not thrive, but equally, if the lights are left on for too long, algae will thrive instead of the plants. If the growth of these microscopic plants begins to develop into a problem, try reducing the length of time that the lights are on.

The risk of algal overgrowth is especially high in an aquarium without live plantsbecause there is no competition with the algae for the nitrate in the water. Some algal growth is natural and will be beneficial in the aquarium, providing a fresh source of food for certain fish, but you need to keep it in check. If algal growth starts to develop on the aquarium glass, remove it using either a magnetic or long-handled cleaner.

Fish-keeping routine

Each day
▶ Check that the fish are eating well. Look for any fish that are off-color or that have died unexpectedly—remove these without delay.
▶ Ensure that all the electrical equipment is functioning correctly. If not, try to find the cause, which may lay outside the aquarium. An air-pump hose might have become kinked after being moved, or a plug might have been inadvertently turned off.

Weekly
▶ Check the levels of ammonia and related nitrogenous chemicals at about the same time. Write the figures down so you can monitor how the filtration system is working.

▶ Monitor the pH in a similar fashion.
▶ Remove any leaves that are obviously dying back, before they begin to decay in the tank.

Monthly
▶ Do a partial water change at least once a month in an established aquarium. Replace the removed water with dechlorinated water of the same temperature, tipping it into the aquarium carefully to avoid disturbing the decor and the fish.
▶ Look for any signs of imminent breeding behaviour in the fish, such as females swelling in size or males becoming more territorial. Transfer breeding fish to a separate breeding tank as necessary.

Take particular care when using a plant fertilizer of any type in a new aquarium. It is more likely to be the algae that will benefit—not the plants.

Aquarium plants

Just as in a garden, you will need to spend some time attending to the needs of the plants for the aquarium to look its best. Plants turning yellow and dying back is common in a new aquarium, but the plants will eventually become established in their new surroundings. Once they do, you may need to divide up clumps of some plants if they begin to take over. You can replant the younger growth, which is likely to be more vigorous. If you add any newly purchased plants, make sure you rinse them off carefully to remove any snail eggs—this is often how snails are introduced to a tank.

Trim off old shoots on a plant that start to turn yellow and die back—this pruning will encourage healthy new growth.

want to know more?

Take it to the next level...

▶ **Fish profiles** 56–165
▶ **Keeping your fish healthy** 168–177

Other sources...

▶ **Specialized aquatic centers: To purchase maintenance equipment and chemicals, such as water conditioners**

▶ **Manufacturers' literature: Follow their specific guidelines for maintaining aquarium equipment, such as filters**

▶ **Fish-keeping magazines: To keep up to date about fish-keeping issues and equipment**

Fish profiles

A wide selection of more than 100 of the most popular aquarium fish are covered in this section. The entries are divided into the main family groupings. Before choosing fish for your tank, check the requirements of individual species carefully—a difference in water chemistry needs, for example, may preclude otherwise compatible species from being kept together.

Anabantoids

The number of anabantoid species has grown significantly in recent years, thanks to the discovery of new species of betta in Indonesia. The group is represented in both Africa and Asia, but it is the Asian species that are the most widely kept and bred.

Surface breathers

These fish often live in shallow, stagnant water in the wild. This water has a low oxygen content, so they have a special labyrinth organ located above the gills on each side of the head. These enable them to come up to the surface to breathe, and the air from the labyrinth organs is absorbed into the bloodstream. If shallow water evaporates, some species can drag themselves over land to pools of water.

In many cases, the males build a nest using bubbles of saliva. However, some bettas are mouthbreeders, with the eggs collected and retained in the mouth of the male fish until the fry hatch. Bubble-nesting types produce thousands of eggs at a single spawning; mouthbreeders, 10 to 50 eggs.

must know

▶ Males can be aggressive toward each other and must not be kept in the same tank, but they may be compatible with other fish.
▶ The long fins of many anabantoids are vulnerable to attack by fin-nipping species, so choose companions carefully. Poor water quality can also lead to infections of the fins.

When breeding bubble-nesting species, such as dwarf gourami *(Colisa lalia)*, do not include a power filter or a similar system that creates a strong current, especially at the water's surface, because it will destroy the nest.

Paradise fish

Macropodus opercularis

These attractive anabantoids are adaptable, being able to survive in unheated water at room temperature, and yet equally able to live in a typical heated aquarium, provided that the water conditions are adjusted gradually. This is a reflection of their natural habitat, because they often live in rice paddies where the shallow water fluctuates markedly in temperature through the day.

Keep the aggressive male fish apart from each other. A male may bully an intended mate, so incorporate a number of retreats in the aquarium, and divide the space with plants and rockwork to provide cover.

Keep the water level shallow, especially for breeding activity, which is triggered by a consistent increase in water temperature.

Male paradise fish have longer fins than females and are also more brightly colored.

The male will build a bubble nest from his own saliva, anchoring it between plants at the surface. Return the female to the main tank after spawning takes place for her own safety. Her mate will collect the eggs, which float at the surface, and transfer them to the nest. The young hatch within a day and become free-swimming about four days later, depending on the water temperature.

data box

FAMILY: Belontiidae
SIZE: 4¾ inches (12cm)
WATER CONDITIONS: Soft and acidic
DISTRIBUTION: Korea, China, and Japan
HABITAT: Rice paddies, slow-flowing water
COMPATIBILITY: Males are aggressive
DIET: Prepared foods and small live foods

Siamese fighting fish
Betta splendens

These stunning anabantoids are so popular that they are often referred to as simply the betta, although there are many other different species of betta. Siamese fighting fish have been selectively bred for centuries in parts of southeast Asia, and they now occur in many different colors. These range from vivid shades of red through blues and violets to black. There is also a whitish variant, known as the Piaket or Cambodian betta, and a yellowish form, too. Fin variants include the crown, which has trailing tips to its fins; the split-tailed, which has a divided caudal fin; and the round-tailed. There are currently more than 100 recognized varieties.

Unfortunately, as their name suggests, male Siamese fighting fish are extremely aggressive by nature. You should never house males together because the weaker male will be killed, and even the survivor may become seriously injured.

Nevertheless, you can house a single male without

problems in a community tank. However, it is important to ensure that there are no similarly colored fish that might be mistaken for another betta in the tank, or it will probably be attacked as a result. For example, if you have a red siamese fighting fish, do not house it with a red-tailed black shark (see page 142).

It is equally important not to include certain species, such as tiger barbs (see page 149), in the same tank, because they will probably nip at the Siamese fighting fish's flowing fins.

Breeding Siamese fighting fish
You are most likely to obtain the best breeding results with fish that are approximately seven months of age.

The female Siamese fighting fish is easy to identify by her small rounded caudal fin.

Siamese fighting fish are easy to sex, thanks to the long, flowing fins of the male that make these fish appealing to fish keepers.

For breeding purposes, house a pair of Siamese fighting fish on their own in an aquarium that contains about 6 inches (15cm) or so of water, with floating plants and gentle filtration.

The male will construct a bubble nest at the surface of the water, then both members of the pair will collect the eggs after spawning, carrying them to the nest. Subsequently, the male will become territorial and drive the female away—at this point you should transfer her back to the main aquarium. The male will remain in the vicinity of the eggs until they hatch about four days later.

Once the eggs hatch, remove the male and rear the young on their own. Their labyrinth organs will become functional once they are about three weeks old. You will be able to identify the male fish from about two months of age onward, at which point you should separate the males from each other.

Siamese fighting fish are generally quite short-lived, with a life expectancy of about two years. Because it is impossible to determine the age of adult fish, it may be better to choose juveniles, particularly for breeding purposes, if these are available.

data box

FAMILY: **Belontiidae**
SIZE: **2 inches (5cm)**
WATER CONDITIONS: **Soft and acidic**
DISTRIBUTION: **Thailand and neighboring countries of southeast Asia**
HABITAT: **Ditches, ponds, rice paddies**
COMPATIBILITY: **Males are highly aggressive**
DIET: **Prepared foods and small live foods**

Croaking gourami
Trichopsis vittata

The croaking calls uttered by these small gouramis are audible when the fish are in breeding condition. They use their swim bladder (a bouyancy organ) to create these sounds, and males are more vocal than females. Sexing based on the appearance of the croaking gourami is difficult, because features, such as natural coloration, can vary slightly between different populations, with some being more brightly colored than others. However, these fish are sociable and you should be able to recognize pairs once they are established in their quarters.

Increasing the water temperature to about 82°F (28°C) can trigger breeding behavior. When such behavior occurs, transfer the pair to a smaller spawning tank

Croaking gouramis are shy by nature, and must be housed in a well-planted aquarium, with subdued lighting.

with floating plants to allow the male to create a bubble nest. Mating takes place beneath the nest, with the eggs floating up and becoming trapped in the bubbles. Females produce less than 200 eggs when spawning. Their rearing requirements are similar to those of other gouramis, with the fry requiring infusoria (microscopic water creatures) or a suitable fry food at first.

data box

FAMILY: **Belontiidae**
SIZE: **2¾ inches (7cm)**
WATER CONDITIONS: **Soft and acidic**
DISTRIBUTION: **Thailand to Sumatra and the Sunda Islands**
HABITAT: **Ditches and ponds**
COMPATIBILITY: **Can be kept with tetras**
DIET: **Prepared foods and small live foods**

Peaceful betta

Betta imbellis

In spite of its common name, males of this species can be aggressive, especially if a new individual is added to an established group.

Although there are regional differences between the various populations, a male peaceful betta can be distinguished from a female by its more colorful appearance. Unlike some bettas, the peaceful betta is a bubble-nesting species. The male will seek out a suitable area between floating plants, which will serve as an anchorage point for the nest. It is at this stage that the reason underlying the common name of this species becomes apparent, because in contrast to the harassing behavior seen in some species, the courtship of this betta is indeed peaceful.

Increasing the amount of live foods in the diet will encourage spawning. It is not uncommon for females to produce several broods of eggs in quite rapid succession. The eggs are laid in groups of about 15 at a time, and the female allows the male to carry them to the nest site after fertilization occurs. The female is likely to lay as many as 150 eggs when she spawns, with this period lasting about two hours in total. The male will guard the nest site, and watches over the young fry at first.

data box

FAMILY: **Belontiidae**
SIZE: **2 inches (5cm)**
WATER CONDITIONS: **Soft, acidic**
DISTRIBUTION: **Malay Peninsula, Phuket, Pinang, Sumatra, Borneo**
HABITAT: **Ditches, ponds, rice paddies**
COMPATIBILITY: **Reasonably social together**
DIET: **Prepared foods and small live foods**

Pearl gourami
Trichogaster leeri

You can sex a pearl gourami once it grows to 3 inches (7.5cm). A male develops a reddish coloration on its underparts, which is more intense when it is in breeding condition. Males are more quarrelsome at this stage. The dorsal fin on the back and the anal fin along the underside of the male's body also develop elongated tips, but these are less conspicuous if the water quality is poor.

A spawning tank at least 3 feet (90cm) long is recommended for a breeding pair—a female pearl gourami can lay 1,000 eggs at a single spawning. Keep the water level in the tank shallow, about 6 inches (15cm) deep, and add floating plants. Incorporate only gentle filtration, such as a foam filter. The plants provide anchorage points for the male gourami to construct a delicate bubble nest, which can be destroyed by a strong current in the tank. Raise the water temperature to 86°F (30°C) to encourage spawning and add additional live foods to the diet to trigger breeding behavior.

Once the bubble nest is almost built,

the male will attract the female to the site and spawning occurs, with the eggs being laid in batches. These are collected by both members of the pair and moved to the nest. The male guards them until the fry emerge and become free-swimming, about three days later. At this stage, move the male back to the main aquarium. To rear the young, feed the fry tiny foods at first.

data box

FAMILY: **Belontiidae**
SIZE: **6 inches (15cm), but often smaller**
WATER CONDITIONS: **Soft, acidic**
DISTRIBUTION: **Southeast Asia, from Thailand to Java and Borneo**
HABITAT: **Rainforest streams**
COMPATIBILITY: **Peaceful**
DIET: **Prepared foods and live foods**

In a community aquarium, choose companions for these fish carefully. Their long fins are a target for fin-nipping species.

Spotted gourami

Trichogaster trichopterus

The appearance of the spotted gourami is variable in terms of both its coloration and its spotted pattern.

The popularity of the spotted gourami has led to a number of different color variants becoming established, including a golden form, and a marbled variety often known as the Cosby. The natural coloration of these fish differs throughout their range, with the bluest individuals occurring on the island of Sumatra. The number of spots on their body may also vary, which is why they may be described as both two- and three-spot gouramis. They are easy to keep but males do not get along, so keep them apart from each other and males of related species.

You can mix pairs with other companions that are nonaggressive, but if you want to breed these gouramis, house them on their own in a relatively large aquarium. The male will build a bulky bubble nest, usually anchoring the structure to floating plants, and will guard both the eggs and fry. As with other bubble-nest builders, never include a power filter in a spawning tank, as it will destroy the delicate nest.

You should remove the female after spawning occurs—otherwise, she may be persecuted by the male. Young spotted gouramis, like related species, have small mouths, so they will require minute rearing foods, such as infusoria, once they become free-swimming.

data box

FAMILY: **Anabantidae**
SIZE: **6 inches (15cm)**
WATER CONDITIONS: **Soft and acidic**
DISTRIBUTION: **Much of southeast Asia**
HABITAT: **Slow-flowing water**
COMPATIBILITY: **Males are aggressive**
DIET: **Prepared foods and small live foods**

Moonlight gourami
Trichogaster microlepis

Sleek in appearance, thanks to its tiny scales, the moonlight gourami is basically a silvery color, aside from the reddish marking on the top half of its iris. The long pelvic fins, located just below the gills in these particular fish, enable them to be sexed. They have a reddish hue in males, but are yellower in females. In contrast, the pectoral fins, which are much more conventionally shaped, are located just behind the gills.

Under no circumstances should these or other related species be accommodated with barbs or other fish that may attack their long, trailing pelvic fins. Tetras will make suitable companions.

Moonlight gourami need a separate aquarium for breeding purposes. You can trigger breeding behavior by lowering the water level and increasing the water temperature slightly to simulate conditions that occur naturally in the wild. You can also increase the amount of live foods in the fish's diet.

The long pelvic fins of the male fish contain receptors, and these pick up chemicals in the water released by the female indicating when she is ready to spawn. A pair will breed using a bubble nest, like other members of this genus.

data box

FAMILY: Anabantidae
SIZE: 6 inches (15cm)
WATER CONDITIONS: Soft and acidic
DISTRIBUTION: Southeastern Asian mainland
HABITAT: Slow-flowing water
COMPATIBILITY: Choose companions carefully
DIET: Prepared foods and small live foods

Moonlight gouramis are shy by nature and require an aquarium setting that provides them with cover.

Dwarf gourami

Colisa lalia

The males have pronounced orange and blue banding on the sides of the body, whereas females have a more silvery appearance.

These beautiful, small gouramis are brightly marked, especially in the case of the male fish. Breeders have also created a range of color varieties, including the popular blue and the red or "sunset" form.

You can keep dwarf gouramis with other non-aggressive fish that have similar water requirements. Even the males of this species will get along reasonably well together, provided that the tank is not overcrowded and it incorporates various retreats, which can be constructed using rockwork and plants.

When setting up a spawning tank for dwarf gouramis, also include aquatic vegetation. This will act as an anchor for the relatively large bubble nest built by the male prior to spawning. Although it is not unknown for a male to mate with more than one female at a time, a pair will often display a strong bond. The male guards the nest on his own. It only takes about a day for the young fry to hatch, although it will be several more days before they are swimming freely around the tank. By this point, make sure you remove both adult fish from the tank—otherwise, they may start to eat their brood.

data box

FAMILY: Belontiidae
SIZE: 2¼ inches (6cm)
WATER CONDITIONS: Soft, acidic
DISTRIBUTION: Parts of northeastern India and Bangladesh
HABITAT: River-drainage systems
COMPATIBILITY: Peaceful
DIET: Prepared foods and live foods

Giant gourami
Colisa fasciata

In spite of its name, the giant gourami does not grow to a massive size. However, be careful that you are not acquiring young specimens of *Osphronemus gorami*, another species that is sometimes confusingly offered under the same common name and that rapidly outgrows the home aquarium. The *Colisa* species is more colorful.

Giant gourami are easy to sex, with males having longer dorsal and caudal fins than females. They require a relatively shallow aquarium, with calm water.

The breeding behavior of the giant gourami does not differ significantly from that of other related species, with the male building a bubble nest at this stage. Once spawning has occurred, allow the male to look after the nest on his own. A single spawning can result in hundreds of fry, so it is important to separate these into groups of similar sizes as they grow larger to prevent overcrowded conditions in the

tank. Otherwise, there is likely to be a marked deterioration in water quality, which can easily result in widespread losses among the fry. Once the young fish reach about 2 inches (5cm) long, you should be able to identify their sex.

> **data box**
>
> FAMILY: **Anabantidae**
> SIZE: **4 inches (10cm)**
> WATER CONDITIONS: **Soft and acidic**
> DISTRIBUTION: **Much of India and Myanmar (Burma)**
> HABITAT: **Slow-flowing water**
> COMPATIBILITY: **Do not mix with fin-nipping fish**
> DIET: **Prepared foods and small live foods**

Male giant gourami can be aggressive toward each other, particularly at spawning time.

Thick-lipped gourami
Colisa labiosa

The reason that these gouramis develop thicker lips is linked with their feeding habits in the wild. Their lips are thick, which helps them to browse on algae that grows on rocks. You can successfully keep a pair with other fish that will not attack their long pectoral fins, but keep males apart as they will fight among themselves.

The male's bubble nest is large, holding as many as 600 eggs, which may be laid at a single spawning, and he may continue expanding the size of the nest afterward.

As in the case of other anabantoids, the young fry will not start to use their labyrinth organs to breathe atmospheric air directly until they are about three weeks old. At this stage it is particularly important to keep the aquarium covered so that the young fish cannot breathe in any airborne pollutants. You should take care to ensure that the water quality is maintained by carrying out partial water changes, and divide the fry into

groups as they grow larger. Check that the water temperature is identical, both when adding fresh water to a tank or when transferring the young fish from one tank to another.

data box

FAMILY: **Anabantidae**
SIZE: **4 inches (10cm)**
WATER CONDITIONS: **Soft and acidic**
DISTRIBUTION: **Northern India, Bangladesh, and Myanmar (Burma)**
HABITAT: **Slow-flowing water**
COMPATIBILITY: **Males are intolerant of each other**
DIET: **Prepared foods, algae, and small live foods**

You can distinguish between the sexes easily—males have more color and a longer dorsal fin.

Kissing gourami
Helostoma temminckii

These anabantoids are so-called because of the way they link their lips together, as if they are kissing. However, this is not a display of affection—it represents a trial of strength, with the weaker individual letting go after a contest that can last for more than 20 minutes. It is thought that this unique behavior may have evolved to minimize the risk of fighting.

In contrast to the somewhat gray form seen in the wild, most kissing gouramis available in aquarium stores are silvery pink, but a mottled variety has also been bred. Sexing these fish is virtually impossible, although mature females may appear broader from behind.

Kissing gouramis are almost entirely vegetarian. This means that they may damage any plants growing in their aquarium, as well as feed on algae and sometimes dig in the substrate.

It is unlikely that you will be able to successfully breed these fish in an aquarium. The male kissing

gourami will not build a bubble nest in such a setting, with the result that the eggs are simply left to float at the surface. This lack of parental concern and nesting restraint may help to explain why a female kissing gourami may lay up to 10,000 eggs when spawning.

data box

FAMILY: Helostomatidae
SIZE: 12 inches (30cm)
WATER CONDITIONS: Soft and acidic
DISTRIBUTION: Thailand, Malaysia, Sumatra, and Borneo
HABITAT: Large areas of water, such as lakes
COMPATIBILITY: Not usually aggressive
DIET: Prepared foods and plant matter

The domesticated silvery pink form of the kissing gourami is most commonly available today.

Catfish

There are over 2,000 different species of catfish, and they represent one of the most diverse groups of aquarium fish. Catfish have a wide distribution, including the loricarids. Those from South America and Africa are popular among fish keepers.

The variable catfish

While some catfish are sedentary, vegetarian bottom-feeders, others are active predators. These hunters hunt other fish after dark, when they are easier to catch. Catfish have sensory projections called barbels around their mouth, which help them to swim safely after dark and find food. The size of the barbels can indicate the behavior of a species—those with long, narrow barbels are more active and predatory. Catfish lack scales, but some have horny body armor.

The loricarids can vary in appearance, and it may be unclear whether a specimen belongs to an existing or an undescribed species. As a result, the "L-numbering" system is used for identifying different varieties, each ascribed a unique number.

must know

▶ Some catfish grow very large. It is vital to determine the adult size of a species before acquiring it to be certain your tank can accommodate it once it is mature.
▶ Catfish are often shy fish, so place retreats in the tank.
▶ Many catfish have spines on their body. Take care when catching them in a net to avoid injury.

Many catfish, such as the spotted pleco (*Hypostomus punctatus*), dig in the substrate in search of edible items. Keep the substrate clean to prevent infections of their barbels and body when they rest here.

Bronze corydoras
Corydoras aeneus

Corydoras catfish will settle well in a community aquarium. They tend to stay relatively close to the bottom of the tank, while other more active fish, such as tetras, swim above them. However, every so often, these catfish will swim up to the surface, where they gulp down a mouthful of air, and then go back down to the bottom again. They store this air in their hindgut, allowing the oxygen to diffuse into the body and supplement the oxygen that they extract from the water through their gills.

The wild coloration of this corydoras catfish is typically a metallic shade of bronze, which is particularly apparent on the sides of the body. However, because of their wide range, there are some differences in their depth of coloration. Breeders have also developed an albino strain of this catfish.

Bronze corydoras have the metallic bronze coloration found on fish in the wild.

Do not rely on these catfish scavenging on leftovers from other fish in the aquarium. Instead, feed these fish special catfish pellets, which will sink quickly to the bottom of the aquarium. They will also eagerly feed on thawed bloodworm and similar live foods, which can help to encourage spawning. Breeding details correspond to those of the peppered corydoras (see opposite).

Albino corydoras are easy to identify by their white coloration and red eyes.

data box

FAMILY: **Callichthyidae**
SIZE: **3 inches (7.5cm)**
WATER CONDITIONS: **Soft, acidic**
DISTRIBUTION: **From Trinidad across northern South America to Brazil**
HABITAT: **Rivers**
COMPATIBILITY: **Peaceful**
DIET: **Prepared foods and live foods**

Peppered corydoras
Corydoras paleatus

This is another popular member of the *Corydoras* group, all of which occur in South America. The peppered corydoras is an adaptable species, which prefers a sandy substrate where it can dig. It is important that this area is kept clean, otherwise the barbels on these fish can become infected.

Sexing is difficult outside the breeding period, when the females swell with eggs. Fortunately, corydoras will live well together, so the likelihood is that you will have at least one pair among a small group.

The breeding habits of the peppered corydoras are similar to those of other species. Lowering the water temperature slightly and doing a partial water change will mimic what happens naturally in the wild after the rains. This will increase the

The peppered corydoras has broad, dark blotches on its body, extending across the fins, and a slight greenish suffusion on the flanks.

likelihood of spawning, which can also be improved by giving them more live foods.

Spawning will occur in the upper part of the breeding tank and may extend over a period of two or three days in total, with up to 300 eggs being laid, usually on the plants. Hatching will take place about five days afterward, at which time the young catfish will require fry food as they become free-swimming.

data box

FAMILY: **Callichthyidae**
SIZE: **3 inches (7.5cm)**
WATER CONDITIONS: **Soft, acidic**
DISTRIBUTION: **Southeastern Brazil, south to La Plata, Argentina**
HABITAT: **Rivers**
COMPATIBILITY: **Peaceful**
DIET: **Prepared foods and live foods**

Green catfish
Brochis splendens

This small catfish looks like a *Corydoras* species in terms of its overall appearance, apart from the fact that its dorsal fin is longer, being made up of more rays. Their requirements are similar, although the green catfish often prefers deeper water.

To help create a naturalistic setting, incorporate a number of retreats on the floor of an aquarium for these catfish. Bogwood is particularly ideal for this purpose. You can keep green catfish in small groups, and they also get along well in a community aquarium.

Sexing is difficult when the age of the fish is unknown. However, as a guide, pick the biggest and smallest fish available, assuming they appear to be healthy.

This popular fish has a distinctive emerald-green body color. It first became available in the 1930s.

Females generally grow significantly larger than males, and their underparts may sometimes have more of a pinkish hue.

The females will lay their eggs on the underside of the broad leaves of aquarium plants, and also among floating plants, producing up to 300 at a single spawning. The young fish will usually hatch about four days later.

data box

FAMILY: Callichthyidae
SIZE: 3 inches (7.5cm)
WATER CONDITIONS: Soft, acidic
DISTRIBUTION: Upper Amazon, in Peru, Ecuador, and Brazil
HABITAT: Rivers
COMPATIBILITY: Peaceful
DIET: Prepared foods and live foods

Armored catfish

Callichthys callichthys

Being nocturnal by nature, armored catfish should be fed at dusk instead of during the daytime with other fish.

These catfish, like *Corydoras* species, have a body casing that consists of a series of interlocking plates covering their bodies like armor. They have relatively small eyes and prominent barbels, which they use both to locate prey and find their way around. Once they are mature, the males of this species can be identified by their thicker pectoral spines.

Armored catfish may sometimes benefit from slightly brackish water conditions, which can be found in estuaries. The adult fish will seek their food at the bottom of the tank, and they will take tablets or pellets, in addition to other items, such as occasional defrosted shrimp.

It is possible to breed this species successfully in a home aquarium. The armored catfish's breeding habits can be fascinating—the male constructs a bubble nest, like many anabantoids.

The female can lay up to 120 eggs at a single spawning. The male will collect the eggs and transfer them to the nest, watching over them until they hatch. The young are easy to rear on a suitable fry food, or even finely powdered egg yolk, with flaked food then being introduced to their diet.

data box

FAMILY: **Callichthyidae**
SIZE: **7¼ inches (18cm)**
WATER CONDITIONS: **Relatively soft, neutral**
DISTRIBUTION: **Much of northern South America**
HABITAT: **From rivers to estuaries**
COMPATIBILITY: **Social, but may prey on smaller fish**
DIET: **Prepared foods and live foods**

Clown peckoltia
Peckoltia vittata

The clown peckoltia is one of the smaller members of its family, with its inoffensive nature making it ideal for a community aquarium of Amazonian fish. Make sure that an aquarium for these nocturnal catfish is well-planted, and incorporate a number of retreats. Bogwood is especially important, because these fish will use their mouthparts to rasp on the wood. They appear to need this in their diet, to keep their digestive system healthy, possibly because it provides dietary fiber.

It is important to feed clown peckoltias at dusk, because this is the time when they normally start to become active. If you feed them during the daytime, you will simply pollute the aquarium, or their food may be

It is not possible to sex the clown peckoltia visually, and virtually nothing is known about their breeding behavior.

eaten by other tank occupants. Clown peckoltias will keep algal growth in check, and ideally it should be present in the aquarium before these fish are introduced to the tank. The algae will make it easier for the fish to acclimatize, because they will have access to a natural food source. Clown peckoltias will not damage plants, nor will they burrow into the base of the aquarium, so they are not disruptive catfish.

data box

FAMILY: **Loricariidae**
SIZE: **4 inches (10cm)**
WATER CONDITIONS: **Soft and acidic**
DISTRIBUTION: **Amazon region of Brazil**
HABITAT: **Rivers**
COMPATIBILITY: **Peaceful**
DIET: **Prepared foods and greenstuff**

Spotted pleco

Hypostomus punctatus

The patterning of the suckermouth varies somewhat between individuals, often reflecting regional differences.

These inoffensive but potentially large catfish are known as suckermouths, thanks to the strong suctionlike mouth that is present on the underside of the body. The mouth parts allow the fish to anchor itself to rockwork or wood underwater, and help to prevent the fish from being swept away by a strong current. They are also used to rasp at bogwood.

Suckermouths are not difficult fish to look after because they are adaptable by nature, but they can be destructive toward the vegetation in an aquarium, uprooting plants even if not actually eating them. Therefore, make sure you choose relatively hardy, fast-growing plant varieties, and set them in pots.

Although these catfish will take tablets readily, they do appreciate fresh foods that they can rasp. Among their favored food items are cucumbers and zucchini, which can be easily provided in the form of individual slices.

Suckermouth catfish will not breed in aquarium surroundings, because they excavate their nesting site in a riverbank to lay their eggs. Therefore, they can only be bred in suitable pond surroundings.

data box

FAMILY: Loricariidae
SIZE: 12 inches (30cm)
WATER CONDITIONS: Soft and acidic
DISTRIBUTION: Southern parts of Brazil
HABITAT: Rivers
COMPATIBILITY: Can be territorial
DIET: Prepared foods and greenstuff

Temminck's bristlenose catfish

Ancistrus temminckii

These small loricariid catfish are ideal occupants for a community aquarium, although they can be territorial toward each other. Adult pairs can be recognized easily, because the male fish develop bristles on its head.

Aside from browsing on algae growing in the aquarium, these catfish feed on a wide range of greenstuff, including fresh peas, red lettuce, and even spinach. In a new aquarium, provide these foods in larger amounts to compensate for the lack of algae. These catfish will also eat small live foods, which are valuable for conditioning.

It is not unknown for a pair to spawn unexpectedly. The eggs are hidden in a suitable cavity, often under rockwork, and

the male guards the eggs and the fry when hatched. Once the young emerge from their hiding places, you can transfer them to a separate tank to rear them on their own, unless the catfish will be the only fish in the aquarium. Algae is valuable as a rearing food for young fish, along with other foods, such as powdered flake.

Shy by nature, Temminck's bristle-nosed catfish become more active after dusk.

> ### data box
>
> **FAMILY:** Loricariidae
> **SIZE:** 5 inches (12.5cm)
> **WATER CONDITIONS:** Soft and acidic
> **DISTRIBUTION:** Much of northern South America
> **HABITAT:** Rivers
> **COMPATIBILITY:** Can be territorial
> **DIET:** Prepared foods and greenstuff

Dwarf sucking catfish
Otocinclus affinis

One of the smallest loricariids, the dwarf sucking catfish is social by nature, and inoffensive toward other tank occupants, making it an ideal choice for a community aquarium. These fish tend to occupy the lower part of the aquarium seeking algae, which forms a major part of their natural diet, although you should supply other alternative sources of greenstuff. These catfish will need a well-planted aquarium. You will also need to make sure that it is effectively filtered to prevent a buildup of dangerous nitrogenous waste.

Females generally have a more rounded appearance than males. Spawning may

Sometimes called the golden otocinclus, its underlying coloration is broken by dark stripes along the sides of the body and speckling over the top of the body.

take place on the plants in the aquarium. If this occurs, transfer the eggs to a separate tank to prevent other aquarium occupants from eating them. The best option is to set up a specific spawning tank. The catfish themselves will not harm their eggs after spawning. Hatching occurs after three days, and you can rear the young on a fry food for egg-layers.

data box

FAMILY: **Loricariidae**
SIZE: **1¼ inches (4cm)**
WATER CONDITIONS: **Soft and acidic**
DISTRIBUTION: **Southeastern Brazil**
HABITAT: **Slow water by banks of streams**
COMPATIBILITY: **Not aggressive**
DIET: **Prepared foods and greenstuff**

Angel catfish
Synodontis angelicus

Synodontis catfish are members of a group known as the naked catfish because they lack the armor associated with other fish belonging to this group. Instead, these catfish have a thick skin, which is covered with mucus to protect them from injury. The even-spotted patterning is most prominent in younger individuals, who are also less gray in color than adults.

Another unusual feature of the angel catfish, and some other species, is the way in which they will swim upside down, although young fish do not behave in this way. It is thought that this strange behavior has developed to enable these catfish to browse on algae that would otherwise be harder for them to reach as they become larger. They also feed in a

The angel catfish is also known as the polka-dot catfish, thanks to the distinctive, even-spotted patterning covering its body.

conventional manner by excavating the substrate in search of edible items.

These catfish become more active at dusk, which is when they prefer to feed. In the home aquarium, this provides a good opportunity to watch them when they are most active, which is especially useful if you have been out at work during the day.

data box

FAMILY: **Mochokidae**
SIZE: **7¼ inches (18cm)**
WATER CONDITIONS: **Relatively soft and acidic**
DISTRIBUTION: **Cameroon and Zaire**
HABITAT: **Slow-flowing, even stagnant water**
COMPATIBILITY: **Not aggressive**
DIET: **Prepared foods, greenstuff, and small live foods**

Banjo catfish
Dysichthys coracoideus

The flattened body shape of these catfish resembles that of the musical instrument, which explains their common name.

The banjo catfish is a bottom-feeder, preferring to live on or near the aquarium substrate. These fish like a sandy base, where they can burrow, decorated with pieces of bogwood, which will provide them with additional cover. In the wild, they often occur in leaf-strewn stretches of water, where the carpet of leaves on the substrate acts as a camouflage and makes them almost invisible. The adult catfish may sometimes prey on aquarium snails, although they will also readily take pellets and hunt out worms.

You can keep banjo catfish in small groups, which will help to increase the chance of breeding success. There is no obvious way of sexing these catfish, until the female starts to swell with eggs and become more rounded in appearance. As the time for breeding approaches, the male banjo catfish will dig a pit in the substrate, which is where spawning takes place, with the female depositing up to 5,000 eggs. These are guarded by the male until they hatch, which occurs about three days later. Rotifers make an ideal rearing food, although you can use a standard fry food as an alternative.

data box

FAMILY: Aspredinidae
SIZE: 5 inches (12.5cm)
WATER CONDITIONS: Relatively soft and acidic
DISTRIBUTION: Amazon basin
HABITAT: Slow-flowing, even stagnant water
COMPATIBILITY: Not aggressive
DIET: Prepared foods and live foods

Angelicus pimelodus

Pimelodus pictus

An obvious feature of the pimelodus pictus (also called the spotted pimelodus) is its long trailing barbels. These fish need to be caught with care because the sharp tips of their pectoral fins can become entangled in the material of the net. It may be much better to use the net simply to steer the fish into a plastic bag filled with water, and then lift it from the aquarium, or scoop out the fish with a clean plastic jug.

Pimelodus pictus get along in groups together or can be housed safely with fish of a similar size. They tend to be nocturnal in their habits; nevertheless, they may be active during the day if the lighting in their

These fish have an attractive dark spotted pattern on their silvery bodies, with pale underparts and blotched markings extending into their dorsal and caudal fins.

quarters is not too bright. A dense covering of floating plants on the surface of the aquarium is recommended for this reason. These catfish also need suitable hiding places in their quarters because they like to retreat into cavelike areas. Make sure you maintain good water conditions. A power filter is important to create a mild current in their quarters.

data box

FAMILY: **Pimelodidae**
SIZE: **6 inches (15cm)**
WATER CONDITIONS: **Soft and acidic**
DISTRIBUTION: **Colombia and Peru**
HABITAT: **Flowing water**
COMPATIBILITY: **Not aggressive**
DIET: **Prepared foods and live foods**

Glass catfish

Kryptopterus bicirrhis

As their name suggests, these catfish are characterized by their transparent bodies, which highlight their skeletal structure.

These catfish can easily blend into their background, and so escape detection. Because they have virtually no dorsal fin, they propel themselves mainly by a combination of their elongated anal fin, which extends along the underside of the body, and their caudal fin. Keep these naturally active catfish in a group of six individuals, with plenty of space for swimming in the aquarium. Place bogwood and plants at the back and along the sides of the tank. Floating plants are also beneficial for these fish.

Their slender barbels, which can almost be as long as their bodies, not only help them find food in the fast-flowing streams which they inhabit, but may also enable them to communicate with each other. It is not unusual for an entire shoal to rest in the water with their heads all pointing in the same direction.

Glass catfish are quite easy to keep, but always check carefully for visible signs of white spot (see page 175) afflicting any of the fish. They are extremely susceptible to this parasitic ailment.

data box

FAMILY: **Siluridae**
SIZE: **6 inches (15cm)**
WATER CONDITIONS: **Soft and acidic**
DISTRIBUTION: **Eastern India across southeast Asia**
HABITAT: **Fast-flowing water**
COMPATIBILITY: **Highly social and not aggressive**
DIET: **Prepared foods and small live foods**

Characiforms

This group includes the popular tetras, which are widely kept in aquaria, as well as the distinctive hatchetfish and some species that will grow to a much larger size, such as the striped anostomus, not to mention the notorious piranhas.

Tetras and their relatives

The characteristics of characiforms as a group are not clear cut, but most have a small adipose fin that can be seen along the top of the lower back, between their dorsal and caudal fins. Virtually all species have teeth that may be as far back as the pharynx in the throat, but their feeding habits are diverse. They range from fearsome carnivores, such as the piranhas to the silver dollar (see page 98) and other *Metynnis* species, which are herbivorous by nature.

Many characiforms display strong shoaling instincts, especially those that tend to be popular in fish-keeping circles, such as the tetras. All are egg layers, and you can often recognize the male fish by their brighter coloration or more elaborate fin shape.

must know

▶ While most tetras are social fish and nonaggressive, not all family members are suitable for community aquaria.
▶ Most members of this group need soft and slightly acidic water conditions, particularly for breeding purposes.
▶ Their eggs may be damaged by light, so do not illuminate the spawning tank.

Rummy-nose tetra *(Hemigrammus bleheri)* is a popular member of the characiforms. Tetras have relatively large eyes, providing them with good vision. Many tetras also have a characteristic colored area on the upper iris of their eyes.

Glass bloodfin

Prionobrama filigera

The body of the glass bloodfin is almost transparent, enabling you to see its internal organs.

Under favorable water conditions and with subdued lighting, the red coloration of the glass bloodfin's caudal fin will be striking. You will need to design an aquarium for glass bloodfins that allows them plenty of swimming space, because these fish are active by nature. Make sure you restrict densely planted areas to the back and sides of the aquarium. If you keep glass bloodfins in small shoals as part of a community aquarium instead of individually, they will be far less nervous.

Sexing these characins presents no difficulty, thanks to the presence of an evident white extension to the anal fin of the male, which is visible along its lower edge. Raising the water temperature as high as 86°F (30°C) and increasing the live food component of the diet will help to trigger spawning behavior. When a pair is ready to spawn, transfer them to a separate tank that includes floating plants. After spawning, move the adult fish back to the main aquarium, leaving the eggs to hatch on their own, which should occur about three days later. You should be able to rear the young quite easily, using a fry food at first.

data box

FAMILY: Characidae
SIZE: 2¼ inches (6cm)
WATER CONDITIONS: Relatively soft and acidic
DISTRIBUTION: Southern Brazil and Argentina
HABITAT: River systems
COMPATIBILITY: Peaceful and social
DIET: Prepared foods and some live foods

Neon tetra
Paracheirodon innesi

You can usually identify the sex of a neon tetra by the bluish stripe that runs along the side of the body. On a female the stripe is slightly broader, and near the tail itself—this stripe is not as straight as in a male. Only purchase the most brightly colored neon tetras; they are susceptible to an untreatable parasitic ailment, which results in loss of coloration in the early stages of their lives. Although it is often known as neon tetra disease, other fish may also be affected. Infected fish can pose a threat to the other occupants of your aquarium.

You can keep neon tetras with other nonaggressive species requiring similar water conditions, such as *Corydoras* catfish (see pages 72–73), which occupy the lower part of the aquarium, and hatchetfish (see page 95), which swim close to the surface. Neon tetras prefer the middle area.

For breeding purposes, you will need to transfer your tetras to a separate tank. Spawning will occur among the aquatic plants, with each female releasing as many as 150 eggs in total. For breeding information, follow the instructions for cardinal tetra (see page 90).

Neon tetras will look best if you keep them in a shoal, in a group of at least five individuals.

data box

FAMILY: **Characidae**
SIZE: **1¾ inches (4cm)**
WATER CONDITIONS: **Soft, acidic**
DISTRIBUTION: **Eastern Peru, South America**
HABITAT: **Shaded waters**
COMPATIBILITY: **Peaceful, shoaling**
DIET: **Prepared foods and live foods**

Blind cave fish
Astyanax jordani

These remarkable fish are found in an underground cave system, where their ancestors became marooned in the past. Living in darkness has led to the loss of both their color pigmentation and eyesight. The young fry still hatch with normal eyes, but skin overgrows them. This leaves them dependent on the sensory input from their lateral line to locate food, avoid danger, and mate.

Although you can keep blind cave fish in a community aquarium with the lighting diffused by a covering of floating plants, you can design a striking recreation of their natural world using calcareous gravel and slate, without any plants. A special night-time fluorescent tube, more commonly

In aquarium surroundings, blind cave fish are just as adept at finding food as other characins that have normal vision.

sold for marine aquaria, will keep the level of illumination low while allowing you to observe the fish.

Keep these fish in groups. Only when the female swells up with her eggs are the sexes discernible. In spite of their lack of vision, the adult fish can still find their eggs and eat them after spawning.

> **data box**
>
> FAMILY: **Characidae**
> SIZE: **4 inches (10cm)**
> WATER CONDITIONS: **Medium hard and alkaline**
> DISTRIBUTION: **San Luis Potosi region of Mexico**
> HABITAT: **Underground rivers**
> COMPATIBILITY: **Can be a fin nipper**
> DIET: **Prepared foods and live foods**

Black neon tetra
Hyphessobrycon herbertaxelrodi

These lively tetras are not a color variant of the neon tetra *(Paracheirodon innesi;* see page 86), but a separate species. They are less colorful, but their true beauty is most apparent when in subdued lighting and good water conditions. If housed in surroundings that are brightly lit, these tetras appear paler than normal, with less contrast between their colors. Black neon tetras do best in small shoals, but you can also mix them with groups of other tetras.

Distinguishing between the sexes is not easy, but the body profile of the female is more rounded. Increasing the amount of live foods in the diet may encourage breeding. Adding a blackwater extract

can help to create more favorable water conditions. Add fine-leaved plants to the spawning tank so the tetras can spawn in the vegetation. After spawning, remove the adult fish. The young fry will start to hatch in two days. They require a fry food at first, then offer them brine shrimp nauplii when about a week old.

data box

FAMILY: **Characidae**
SIZE: **2 inches (5cm)**
WATER CONDITIONS: **Soft and acidic**
DISTRIBUTION: **Taquari River, Mato Grosso, Brazil**
HABITAT: **Tributary of the Paraguay River**
COMPATIBILITY: **Social**
DIET: **Prepared foods and live foods**

Black neon tetras have a black area running beneath a golden-green stripe, which extends down each side of the body.

Lemon tetra
Hyphessobrycon pulchripinnis

Like many tetras, these fish have a bright red area above the pupils of the eyes. Lemon tetras should not be confused with the yellow tetra *(H. bifasciatus)*, which lacks this evident reddish marking, and also the yellow and black streaking present at the front of their anal and dorsal fins.

Keep lemon tetras in a well-planted aquarium that mimics their natural habitat, with some open areas where the fish can shoal and swim freely as a group. These tetras prefer the middle region of the aquarium, so they are compatible with hatchetfish, for example, which remain close to the surface, and small catfish, such as corydoras, which swim beneath them.

The silvery yellow coloration of the lemon tetra is apparent on the lower surface of the body—males are more colorful than females.

Lemon tetras are easy to breed in the home aquarium if their spawning tank does not have a light, which can damage the eggs and prevent hatching. These tetras prefer to spawn among fine-leaved plants. After spawning, remove the adult fish immediately afterward—otherwise, the adults are likely to eat their eggs.

data box

FAMILY: **Characidae**
SIZE: **2 inches (5cm)**
WATER CONDITIONS: **Soft and acidic**
DISTRIBUTION: **Ranges quite widely through the Amazon basin**
HABITAT: **Mainly found in streams**
COMPATIBILITY: **Social**
DIET: **Prepared foods and live foods**

Cardinal tetra
Paracheirodon axelrodi

Peaceful by nature, brightly colored cardinal tetras are easy to keep. Their only special requirement is diffused lighting over their tank, which you can achieve by including floating plants at the surface. Keep cardinal tetras in shoals because this is how they live in the wild.

A shoal of tetras obviously increases the possibility of breeding. However, the cardinal tetra is not an easy tetra to spawn successfully in aquarium surroundings. Feed these fish small live foods, such as whiteworm, as a breeding conditioner. Prior to spawning, you may be able to distinguish the female fish as they develop a more rotund appearance. You will need a

The red stripe that runs along the entire underside of the cardinal tetra serves to distinguish it from its near relative, the neon tetra *(Paracheirodon innesi)*.

separate breeding tank, but as soon as spawning occurs, usually toward dusk, remove the adults before they eat the eggs.

Do not illuminate the breeding tank, because lighting significantly reduces the viability of the eggs. Hatching will take place about a day later. You will need to provide a special fry food for the young tetras as soon as they are free-swimming.

data box

FAMILY: **Characidae**
SIZE: **2 inches (5cm)**
WATER CONDITIONS: **Soft, acidic**
DISTRIBUTION: **Northwestern South America**
HABITAT: **Shaded waters**
COMPATIBILITY: **Peaceful, shoaling**
DIET: **Prepared foods and live foods**

Black widow tetra

Gymnocorymbus ternetzi

Black widow tetras have three black vertical bars running down each side of their body.

You can assess the age of these tetras by their patterning, which is less distinctive on young fish. The color of the anal fin is blackish at first, turning grayish by about a year old. Sexing is fairly simple, because the anal fin is longer at the front in males and females have a more rounded body shape.

Black widows originate from further south than many tetras and make an ideal introduction to the group. There is also a long-finned strain of these fish, which are popular among fish keepers. A shoal of naturally active black widows are not suitable for an aquarium accommodating more nervous companions—these are boisterous fish, although not aggressive.

You should separate the females from a group about a week prior to spawning. Feed them live foods, such as mosquito larvae. The spawning tank should contain fine-leaved vegetation, where the eggs will be laid and will tend to stick. Afterward, transfer the adult tetras back to the main aquarium, and rear the young fish on fry food once they hatch.

data box

FAMILY: **Characidae**
SIZE: **2 inches (5cm)**
WATER CONDITIONS: **Soft and acidic**
DISTRIBUTION: **Parts of southern Brazil, Bolivia, and Paraguay**
HABITAT: **Rivers with tall vegetation**
COMPATIBILITY: **Social**
DIET: **Prepared foods and live foods**

Glowlight tetra
Hemigrammus erythrozonus

The reddish-golden stripe that runs down the sides of the body of the glowlight tetra has a luminous quality. This fish also has a reddish mark at the front of the dorsal fin, the shape of which often allows individuals in a shoal to be identified. The glowlight tetra is active by nature and conspicuous, especially once it has settled in its surroundings. It prefers visiting open areas instead of skulking among the vegetation. Females are recognizable by their deeper bodies and slightly larger size.

A separate tank will be necessary for spawning. Eggs are laid among plants, such as *Myriophyllum*, and as many as 200 eggs may be produced by a single female.

Glowlight tetras will thrive in a small group as part of a community aquarium featuring fish of Amazonian origins.

Rearing the young fry is not difficult, but they will require tiny particles of food. If cultures of microscopic water creatures known as infusoria are not available, feed them a commercially available rearing food sold for the fry of egg layers. You can gradually introduce flaked food to their diet as they grow by rubbing it between your fingers to create smaller powdered particles.

data box

FAMILY: **Characidae**
SIZE: **2 inches (5cm)**
WATER CONDITIONS: **Soft and acidic**
DISTRIBUTION: **Essequibo basin of Guyana**
HABITAT: **Rivers with aquatic vegetation**
COMPATIBILITY: **Social**
DIET: **Prepared foods and live foods**

Rummy-nose tetra
Hemigrammus bleheri

There is often confusion between this species and the similar red-nosed tetra (*H. rhodostomus*), which is also sometimes described as the rummy-nose tetra. The simple way to distinguish between them is that *H. bleheri* has a more extensive area of red coloration on the head, extending back to the body, and it lacks any black markings on the anal fin seen on *H. rhodostomus*.

Both these tetras need similar care and can be sensitive to water quality. You'll need to make regular water changes to ensure that the nitrate level remains low. It is equally important to avoid overfeeding, because any uneaten food will simply decay and pollute the tank.

The rummy-nosed tetra is more likely to breed when a group of them are kept in a spawning tank together instead of only a single pair.

To trigger spawning behavior, use a blackwater extract or filter the water through aquarium peat to create similar water conditions under which these fish live in the wild. Small live foods, such as gnat larvae, can encourage breeding. Include marbles on the base of the tank to reduce the risk of the eggs being eaten as they are laid.

data box

FAMILY: **Characidae**
SIZE: **2 inches (5cm)**
WATER CONDITIONS: **Soft and acidic**
DISTRIBUTION: **Rio Vaupés in Colombia and the Rio Negro, Brazil**
HABITAT: **Rivers with aquatic vegetation**
COMPATIBILITY: **Social**
DIET: **Prepared foods and live foods**

X-ray tetra
Pristella maxillaris

If you keep X-ray tetras in a brightly lit aquarium, the subtle coloration of these fish will be obscured, with only their black markings being clearly visible. In addition, the red of their caudal fin and the yellow area on the dorsal fin will appear washed out and be barely discernible.

A temporary high level of illumination will help you to determine the sex of the fish. However, because X-ray tetras are best kept in groups, establishing the sexes will be less important when compared to aquarium fish that need to be kept in pairs.

You can also keep X-ray tetras as part of a community aquarium with other types of nonaggressive fish. This will offer you the opportunity to create a "themed tank," incorporating plants and other fish that are likely to be found alongside X-ray tetras in the wild in the Amazon region, such as the glowlight tetra (see page 92) and marbled hatchetfish (see opposite). Along with subdued illumination, a dark substrate in the aquarium will help to highlight the natural subtleties of the tetra's coloration.

Once the fish are established in their quarters, you can trigger spawning by raising the water temperature to 84°F (29°C) and using a blackwater extract. Increasing the amount of live foods in their diet can also help to encourage spawning behavior.

data box

FAMILY: Characidae
SIZE: 2 inches (5cm)
WATER CONDITIONS: Relatively soft and acidic
DISTRIBUTION: Venezuela, Guyana, and Brazil
HABITAT: Slow-flowing waters in the Amazon region
COMPATIBILITY: Social, associating in shoals
DIET: Prepared foods and some live foods

The semitransparent nature of their bodies highlights the internal organ known as the swim bladder, which has a more rounded shape in females.

Marbled hatchetfish

Carnegiella strigata

The pattern on the body of the marbled hatchetfish will enable individual fish in a shoal to be distinguished easily.

Hatchetfish are so-called because of the shape of their body, with the underside of the body being curved and resembling the sharp edge of an ax. The top line of the hatchetfish is relatively flat, and its mouth is upturned. These features typically indicate a group of fish that live near to and feed at the surface.

The hatchetfish's body is remarkably aerodynamic, to the extent that these fish will naturally leap out of the water to catch a passing insect or glide some distance to avoid a predator. Therefore, it is vital to keep their aquarium covered at all times to prevent them from jumping out of the tank. By including floating plants at the surface, you will provide these fish with a greater sense of security, making them less inclined to behave in this manner.

Before purchasing marbled hatchetfish, make sure you check the fish carefully for signs of white spot (see page 175). These fish seem to be particularly vulnerable to this parasitic disease.

Hatchetfish are insectivorous by nature. They will benefit from a diet that includes insects such as fruit flies or tiny crickets.

data box

FAMILY: **Characidae**
SIZE: **2 inches (5cm)**
WATER CONDITIONS: **Soft and acidic**
DISTRIBUTION: **Northern South America**
HABITAT: **Rivers with floating aquatic vegetation**
COMPATIBILITY: **Social**
DIET: **Prepared foods and surface insects**

Striped anostomus

Anostomus anostomus

This is one of a number of fish whose common name directly reflects their scientific name. However, it also has an alternative common name—the striped headstander. This describes both its appearance and the way in which the fish will float in the water at an angle, with its head pointing downward, while it feeds on algae.

The striped anostomus grows to a relatively large size, and it is usually less aggressive if kept in groups, so a spacious aquarium is recommended for a number of these fish instead of housing only two together. Unfortunately, it is impossible to determine the sexes by their appearance, but breeding in aquarium surroundings is very unlikely in any case.

Striped anostomus originate from relatively fast-flowing stretches of water, where pollutants do not accumulate in the water, so it is important that an aquarium for these fish incorporates an efficient filtration system. Make sure you carry out partial water changes as necessary. In addition, there should be a high level of illumination in the tank to encourage the growth of algae on rockwork and other tank decor, because this will feature prominently in the diet of these fish.

data box

FAMILY: **Anostomidae**
SIZE: **7¼ inches (18cm)**
WATER CONDITIONS: **Relatively soft and acidic**
DISTRIBUTION: **Northern areas of South America**
HABITAT: **Rapid-flowing stretches of water**
COMPATIBILITY: **Often proves aggressive**
DIET: **Prepared foods, plant matter, and some live foods**

This fish uses its prominent lower jaw to pluck at the algae, causing it to feed upside down.

Marbled headstander
Abramites hypselonotus

In contrast to most fish, where drifting at an abnormal angle is a sign of serious ill-health, such behavior is a feature of headstanders as a group. As they age the appearance of marbled headstanders alters. They develop a broader back, which explains their alternative name of high-backed headstander.

These fish are not social by nature, which means that you will probably need to keep them individually, unless the aquarium is large and well-planted. However, they will agree well with unrelated fish in a community aquarium even when adult.

If frightened, marbled headstanders will dart straight upward and can jump out of the tank, so you will need to keep them in a covered aquarium. These fish are quite nervous by nature, so incorporating a covering of floating plants at the surface will provide the headstander with reassurance. Duckweed (*Lemna* species) will be valuable to the fish, because it also helps to supplement the

headstander's diet. Make sure you choose other plants for the headstander's aquarium carefully, generally restricting them to tough, fast-growing species. Otherwise, the plants are likely to be eaten by these fish.

> **data box**
>
> FAMILY: **Anostomidae**
> SIZE: **5¼ inches (13.5cm)**
> WATER CONDITIONS: **Soft and acidic**
> DISTRIBUTION: **Amazon and Orinoco river basins**
> HABITAT: **Flowing water**
> COMPATIBILITY: **Not social**
> DIET: **Prepared foods, greenstuff, and live foods**

You can provide hiding places for the nervous marble headstander by adding plastic plants to the tank, along with bogwood and similar retreats.

Silver dollar

Metynnis argenteus

The individual appearance of these fish can differ quite widely in terms of their depth of silvery coloration, reflecting differences in the ancestral stocks of today's aquarium strains. In fact, more than one type of fish is known under this common name, adding to the confusion. However, in all cases the care of these fish is similar.

The silver dollar needs a more spacious aquarium, where a school of these fish can look stunning. Silver dollars must have plenty of open swimming space, but they also require retreats constructed using rockwork and bogwood, where they can lurk on occasions out of sight. Without these areas, the fish can display much more nervous behavior.

The aquarium lighting should be relatively subdued, and because silver dollars will eat vegetation in their quarters, include only tough, fast-growing plants in the tank. It may be possible to deter the fish from browsing on the plants by supplementing their diet with items, such

as fresh lettuce leaves—choose organic lettuce, which will be free from chemicals. For spawning purposes, grow plants such as Java moss *(Vesicularia dubyana)*, which these fish are less likely to eat. Mating will occur among the plant's fronds.

data box

FAMILY: **Characidae**
SIZE: **5½ inches (14cm)**
WATER CONDITIONS: **Soft and acidic**
DISTRIBUTION: **The Guianas to the Amazon basin**
HABITAT: **Rivers with floating aquatic vegetation**
COMPATIBILITY: **Social**
DIET: **Mainly vegetable-based diets and fresh greenstuff**

The silver dollar grows to a larger size than the tetras that are common in this family.

Cichlids

One of the most popular groups of all aquarium fish is the cichlids. However, this is an aggressive group, so cichlids tend to be housed in pairs or groups on their own, and many species are unsuitable for a community aquarium.

The aggressive cichlids

Cichlids can grow large, and they may be predatory in their feeding habits. Keeping a number of them in a tank can be disruptive, where they dig up the substrate and plants.

Certain cichlids, notably the discus (see page 100-1) and angelfish (see pages 104-5), have been bred in many color varieties. Rare forms of the discus can be expensive.

Some cichlids lay eggs in the open or in caves, watching over them and the fry once they hatch. In other cases, parental care has progressed, with the female fish collecting and carrying her eggs in her mouth for two weeks or so, until they hatch. Only then will she start to feed again, but she still allows her offspring to dart back into her mouth if danger threatens.

must know

▶ Cichlids vary in terms of the water conditions that they require. Those from the Amazon region require soft and acidic water; those from the East African lakes like hard, alkaline waters. Adjust your water accordingly.
▶ Discover as much as possible about a species that appeals to you—some can grow to a large size.

Aggression between males is likely in many species, including the firemouth cichlid *(Cichlasoma meeki)*. As they grow older separate a group into individual pairs to prevent fighting. Some males can injure females when spawning.

Discus
Symphysodon discus

These cichlids are so-called because of their circular body shape, resembling that of a discus, although up until six months of age, they have a more elongated profile. Discus rank as the most popular of all cichlids, but they can be expensive.

Today's discus are far removed from their wild ancestors—they have been selectively bred for their coloration and patterning. The commercially bred fish are more brightly colored than their wild relatives, although these fish do display distinctive regional variations, and green, brown, and bluish strains can be identified from specific localities across their wide range.

A second, more localized species, called Heckel's discus *(S. discus)* has also contributed to the strains being bred today. You can see its influence in the broad, dark-colored "Heckel band" that runs vertically down the center of the fish's body.

Discus have special requirements when it comes to keeping them in an aquarium. They are also more difficult to keep if you live in a hard-water area, because they need soft-water conditions. Because of their height, they also require a relatively deep aquarium. In addition, they will benefit from the addition of a blackwater extract.

If you purchase these fish when they are approximately 4 inches (10cm) long, it will be possible to sex them with some certainty. It is usually better to start with young discus, rather than introducing two or more adults together—the adults are

The striking coloration is an appealing feature of the discus, some of which have signs of a dark-colored vertical "Heckel band."

The male discus develops a hump on the forehead as he matures—the female's profile is more rounded.

less likely to be compatible for breeding purposes. Alternatively, you can keep a group of discus in a large aquarium together, allowing them to form pairs among themselves. The pairs will swim together, remaining in relatively close contact with each other at all times. Eventually, you should be able to recognize a particular fish by its individual head patterning, which will make it easier to identify a pair when transferring them elsewhere for breeding purposes.

Discus need a spawning surface, such as a piece of slate in their aquarium, which they will clean carefully before the female deposits up to 400 eggs on it. Be sure to use a safe heater guard, which will allow the water to circulate around the heater, but will prevent the female laying on the casing where the eggs will be destroyed.

After spawning, both parents will remain nearby and watch over their eggs. It is important to leave them alone at this stage, because if disturbed, they may actually eat the eggs. This can sometimes happen with young pairs, but ultimately,

they should prove to be excellent parents, even helping the fry out of the eggs and carrying them to aquatic plants nearby.

The fry will become free-swimming once they are about five days old. At first, they will feed on mucus produced by the parents on their flanks, which is known as "discus milk."

data box

FAMILY: **Cichlidae**
SIZE: **8 inches (20cm)**
WATER CONDITIONS: **Relatively soft and acidic**
DISTRIBUTION: **Throughout the Amazon region**
HABITAT: **River systems**
COMPATIBILITY: **Peaceful and social**
DIET: **Special discus food and some live foods**

Oscar

Astronotus ocellatus

The oscar is a particularly popular member of the cichlid group. It grows to a relatively large size and will require a correspondingly spacious aquarium. An oscar can become friendly, even recognizing its owner and taking food from the hand. If you want to encourage an oscar to behave in this manner, it is better to start with a young fish, which can be tamed more easily than an adult. Oscars are far less colorful when young, with a different pattern of markings. These consist of dark and light areas of marbling, but without the obvious reddish-orange areas that are a feature typically seen on an adult.

Young oscars lack the characteristic orange-bordered dark spot at the base of the caudal peduncle near the tail, which is seen in adults.

The actual patterning of oscars differs widely, with some individuals displaying more extensive orange coloration than others as they grow older. This is probably a reflection of the differences apparent in wild populations, which are widely distributed through northern South America. Captive-breeding has focused on developing strains with bright orange-red coloration, which can be further emphasized by feeding these fish color foods. There are also striped and albino oscars. Domestication of these fish has also resulted in the creation of long-finned oscars, but these have not become especially popular.

It is not possible to sex oscars until they are in breeding condition, when females

In the albino oscar, the dark background color has been replaced by white coloration, leaving the reddish areas unaffected.

develop swellings known as genital papillae close to the vent. They can start spawning when they are about 4½ inches (11cm) long. The courtship itself can be aggressive, but oscars normally form a strong bonding pair. In fact, they may be able to recognize each other by their markings, just as they can identify their owner.

A clay flowerpot is an ideal spawning site, or carefully position a well-supported piece of slate for the same purpose. A female lays about 1,000 eggs, which are then guarded by the adult fish. After three days, when the young hatch, their parents herd them to a hollow dug into the aquarium substrate, where they will continue to watch over them. It is also quite usual for oscars to excavate the substrate on a regular basis in search of edible items.

The red tiger strain has distinctive reddish stripes over its body instead of only isolated orange areas.

data box

FAMILY: Cichlidae
SIZE: 14 inches (35cm)
WATER CONDITIONS: Soft and acidic
DISTRIBUTION: Parts of the Paraguay, Orinoco and Amazon rivers
HABITAT: Rivers
COMPATIBILITY: Best housed individually or in pairs
DIET: Prepared foods and bigger live foods

Angelfish
Pterophyllum scalare

These distinctive cichlids, with their tall, flattened body shape, are popular among fish enthusiasts, and they are occasionally recommended for a community aquarium when young. Unfortunately, they often do not thrive in these surroundings, because their long, trailing fins are frequently attacked by other fish sharing their accommodation. Conversely, their rate of growth is often much faster than that of the other aquarium occupants, and when they are larger the angelfish may retaliate by persecuting their companions instead.

If you want to keep these elegant fish, it is better to set up an aquarium specifically for a small shoal of them. Select a tank that is relatively deep to take account of the fish's unusual shape. You should dedicate an area of the tank to a group of tall plants, such as straight vallis (*Vallisneria spiralis*), which will reveal the reason behind the angelfish's distinctive profile. These fish are able to swim easily through heavily vegetated areas of water,

weaving between reedy plants and disappearing from would-be predators.

Keeping a group of angelfish together also enhances the likelihood that you will have a true pair, because it is impossible to sex them visually. They are easy to breed, and this helps to explain the wide range of color forms that now exist. There are three distinctive types of angelfish recognized from the wild, distinguished in part on the basis of their head shape,

The gold-headed angelfish has a golden color restricted to the head. On other variants, this color is evident over the entire body.

although these have now been quite widely interbred, so most aquarium stock tends to have hybrid origins.

Among the most commonly seen colur variants are golden strains of angelfish. At the other extreme, black angelfish now exist, which lack the lighter silvery brown areas found on other types. There are also angelfish where patterning is still present, but far removed from that of the wild fish, as typified by the marbled varieties. Fin variants have also occurred, for instance resulting in veil-tailed strains, where the tail fin has a more elaborate appearance.

Once a pair forms a bond, with the fish staying close together, move them to an aquarium on their own. They will choose

The blushing golden angelfish is among the most popular color variants of the golden strains of angelfish.

a spawning site, such as a piece of slate, and the female will clean the area by nibbling at it before laying up to 1,000 eggs. In the case of pairs breeding for the first time, they may eat their eggs; however, the female should lay again within a few weeks with a successful result. The young angelfish are guarded by their parents, and they are restricted at first to a pit that has been dug in the substrate for them.

Because the long fins on the angelfish are susceptible to attack by other fish, it is best to keep them in a separate tank.

data box

FAMILY: Cichlidae
SIZE: 6 inches (15cm)
WATER CONDITIONS: Soft, acidic
DISTRIBUTION: Throughout the Amazon
HABITAT: Slow-flowing, well-vegetated waters
COMPATIBILITY: Peaceful
DIET: Prepared foods and live foods

Convict cichlid
Archocentrus nigrofasciatum

The striped markings of these cichlids resemble the traditional patterning on the uniform of convicts. Convict cichlids are easy to look after, but they are quite aggressive by nature, and therefore, it is better to keep pairs on their own.

You can identify the females by the orange suffusion on their underparts, while mature males often develop a slight hump on the head. As the time for spawning approaches, the gray areas of their body become whiter. This loss of color is not a sign of ill-health, which is often the case with other fish. You'll find a clay flowerpot is useful as a spawning site in the tank.

Make sure you design the planting scheme for an aquarium with a pair of convict cichlids takes into account their destructive nature. They will dig in the substrate, uprooting plants and eating them, too. Setting the plants in small containers,instead of rooting them in the substrate can help, while choosing tough, rapid-growing

specimens, such as vallisneria, is also recommended. Offering the cichlids some fresh greenstuff as part of their regular diet can be beneficial by distracting them away from the aquatic vegetation—however, they generally prefer live foods.

data box

FAMILY: **Cichlidae**
SIZE: **6 inches (15cm)**
WATER CONDITIONS: **Soft and acidic**
DISTRIBUTION: **Central America, from Guatemala to Panama**
HABITAT: **Rivers and streams**
COMPATIBILITY: **Best housed individually or as true pairs**
DIET: **Prepared foods, live foods, and greenstuff**

The stripes on the body of the convict cichlid breaks up their outline, which helps to protect them from potential predators in the wild.

Ram

Mikrogeophagus ramirezi

The male ram is significantly larger than a female, and he has a larger dorsal fin than his mate.

The delicate appearance of this cichlid has led to it also being known as the butterfly dwarf cichlid. As domestication has proceeded, these fish have become more colorful, with a golden variety now also being well-established.

There is a variance in size between the sexes, with the male being larger. Male rams lack the reddish area seen on the underparts of females, which darkens as they come into breeding condition. It is important to be able to sex these cichlids even if you do not want to breed them, because the males are territorial and aggressive by nature toward each other, and you should not house them together.

An aquarium for these cichlids needs to have well-planted areas, and also some open stretches of water, where a pair may decide to spawn on rockwork. However, the female may prefer to spawn in a hole dug in the aquarium substrate. Her eggs are red in color, and they may number up to 200 in total. Breeding pairs are often prolific, especially if housed in favorable conditions, spawning on a monthly basis once mature.

data box

FAMILY: Cichlidae
SIZE: 3 inches (7.5cm)
WATER CONDITIONS: Soft and acidic
DISTRIBUTION: Rio Meta in Colombia and the Orinoco in Venezuela
HABITAT: Flowing water and savannah pools
COMPATIBILITY: Best housed individually or as true pairs
DIET: Prepared foods and live foods

Agassiz's dwarf cichlid
Apistogramma agassizi

The appearance of these cichlids varies quite markedly throughout their natural distribution. Today's most brightly colored strains have been developed from red-tailed populations occurring in western parts of their range. In all cases, males can be identified by their larger size, with their caudal fin being more elongated, rather than rounded as in females.

Good water quality is important to the well-being of these cichlids. In the wild, these fish are used to the quieter parts of fast-flowing waters, but where pollutants cannot accumulate, so you will need to do regular partial water changes and monitor the water to keep nitrate levels low.

A single male can be housed with one or more females, although you will need to divide the tank with plants and rockwork to ensure that each fish has adequate space to prevent conflicts. Spawning usually takes place on the underside of flowerpots or in similar secluded areas, mimicking the small caves and rocky overhangs that these cichlids use in the wild.

A female can lay up to 150 eggs in a batch, and she will watch over the fry when they hatch four days later. It will be another four days before they will be swimming freely. Rear the young cichlids on brine shrimp nauplii, and separate them into small groups as they grow.

data box

FAMILY: **Cichlidae**
SIZE: **3 inches (7.5cm)**
WATER CONDITIONS: **Soft and acidic**
DISTRIBUTIONS: **Tributaries of the Amazon river**
HABITAT: **River systems**
COMPATIBILITY: **Males are likely to be combative**
DIET: **Prepared foods and live foods**

Agassiz's dwarf cichlid has a dark brown line that runs along its side from the tail to the eye. Some scales have an appealing metallic sheen.

Firemouth cichlid

Amphilophus macracanthus

Besides having a more colourful red throat, a firemouth male can be identified by the trailing tips of its dorsal and anal fins.

The striking red throat of the firemouth cichlid may appear attractive to our eyes, but it actually serves as a signal to other firemouths. When inflated, it acts as a threatening gesture to intimidate a potential rival and also forms part of its courtship ritual. The red coloration is most evident in males, and can be emphasized by feeding the fish a special food for enhancing fish color.

Like many Central American cichlids, the firemouth will dig keenly in the substrate, seeking edible items, and creating spawning pits, where its young can be corralled after hatching to keep them relatively safe. It is a good idea to provide them with a sandy substrate in the tank and to set any aquarium plants in pots

to prevent them being dislodged by the burrowing behavior of these cichlids.

Keep pairs on their own for spawning purposes—however, you may need to remove the male temporarily if he starts to persecute his intended mate. A female may lay up to 500 eggs on smooth rock or slate.

data box

FAMILY: Cichlidae
SIZE: 6 inches (15cm)
WATER CONDITIONS: Medium hard and neutral
DISTRIBUTION: Guatemala and Mexico
HABITAT: River systems
COMPATIBILITY: Males are aggressive
DIET: Prepared foods and live foods

Jewel cichlid
Hemigrammus species

In spite of their attractive appearance, you will need to keep a pair of jewel cichlids on their own because these fish are aggressive by nature. When introducing a pair of these fish together, place them in the aquarium at the same time to minimize any conflict. You can remove an established individual and readjust the decor in the tank to avoid giving either member of the pair any territorial advantage.

Jewel cichlids are destructive by nature, and you will need to consider this aspect of their behavior when planning the design of an aquarium for them. Plants are likely to be dug up because these fish regularly forage in the substrate for food. However, it may be possible to overcome this problem by protecting the base of plants with large pebbles. Use larger rocks to create retreats that will give the female protection from her partner before spawning begins. These cichlids become particularly colorful at this stage, with the red areas on their bodies becoming more intense. The eggs are laid on a rock, and the young cichlids are guarded by their parents after hatching.

The jewel cichlid is an attractive fish covered with iridescent spots, which suggested the name for this fish.

data box

FAMILY: Cichlidae
SIZE: 6 inches (15cm)
WATER CONDITIONS: Soft and acidic
DISTRIBUTION: West Africa, from southern Guinea to central Liberia
HABITAT: Mainly streams
COMPATIBILITY: Keep as pairs on their own
DIET: Prepared foods and live foods

Lemon cichlid

Lamprotogus leleupi

The huge areas of freshwater lakes of Africa's Rift Valley are home to thousands of diverse species of cichlid. The lemon cichlid is an attractive species, which varies in its depth of coloration in different parts of its range. Those found in the northwest part of Lake Tanganyika are the darkest, being orange-brown instead of yellowish.

You should keep pairs on their own because they are aggressive by nature. The male can be recognized by his longer pelvic fins. In the wild, lemon cichlids will spawn in underwater caves, which provide a relatively safe retreat for them. In aquarium surroundings, they will use a clean clay flowerpot as a substitute. The female will lay around 150 eggs, while the male will guard the entrance to their nest site.

You may deepen the yellow coloration on a lemon cichlid by feeding it special food, which enhances its color.

Their young need a fry food at first and will continue to be watched over by their parents. However, you should remove the young fish to separate accommodation before the adult pair spawn again, which may be as soon as six weeks later. The young themselves are normally capable of breeding within 18 months.

data box

FAMILY: **Cichlidae**
SIZE: **4 inches (10cm)**
WATER CONDITIONS: **Hard and alkaline**
DISTRIBUTION: **Lake Tanganyika in East Africa**
HABITAT: **Along both the western and eastern shorelines**
COMPATIBILITY: **Keep them as pairs on their own**
DIET: **Prepared foods and live foods**

Malawi golden cichlid
Melanochromis auratus

The name of these cichlids can be confusing because only the female displays the golden yellow area running along the underside of her body, with brown and silvery striping above. The male Malawi golden cichlid is dramatically different in color, being much darker overall with pale sky blue striping on the sides of his body, although there are some regional differences in appearance. It is important to always keep a male with several females on their own in order to maintain harmony, because a single female is likely to be persecuted, as will any other fish in the tank.

These cichlids are found along the rocky shoreline of lakes in the wild, so you should provide them with plenty of retreats in their quarters. The aquarium will also need to be

The darker male Malawi golden cichlid has a blue stripe along the sides of his body—the female is the one with golden yellow coloration.

relatively well lit, to encourage the growth of algae on the rocks, which the cichlids can browse on just as they do in the wild.

When breeding, a female collects her eggs in her mouth and keeps them there until the young cichlids hatch. This mouthbreeding behavior restricts the number of eggs that she lays to a maximum of about 30. She will not eat until her young hatch after about three weeks.

data box

FAMILY: **Cichlidae**
SIZE: **5 inches (12.5cm)**
WATER CONDITIONS: **Hard and alkaline**
DISTRIBUTION: **Lake Malawi in East Africa**
HABITAT: **Relatively shallow water**
COMPATIBILITY: **Males are aggressive**
DIET: **A prepared cichlid diet for vegetarian species**

Tropheops

Pseudotropheus tropheops

The darker male tropheops frequently displays a metallic bluish suffusion on its flanks.

Like the Malawi golden cichlid, this is a polygamous cichlid species, meaning that a single male needs to be housed with a group of several females. Sexing on the basis of their coloration is reasonably straightforward, because males are much darker in color than females. These cichlids belong to the so-called "mbuna" group. This description is a local name that means "rock-dwelling," and it refers to the type of habitat close to the shore of the lake where tropheops are found.

The water requirements of this species and other Rift Valley cichlids are different from those found in Amazonian regions. This impacts the choice of aquarium plants for their quarters, especially as they are a herbivorous species. Choose tough, fast-growing vegetation, such as vallisnerias and Java moss (*Vesicularia dubyana*).

Tropheops is a mouthbreeding species, and a female will continue to display protective behavior toward her brood even after they have hatched and left the safety of her mouth. If danger threatens, she will simply open her mouth, allowing the young cichlids to swim back inside for about a week after they first emerge.

data box

FAMILY: Cichlidae
SIZE: 6 inches (15cm)
WATER CONDITIONS: Hard and alkaline
DISTRIBUTION: Southern end of Lake Malawi in East Africa
HABITAT: Relatively shallow water
COMPATIBILITY: Males are aggressive
DIET: A prepared cichlid diet with a vegetable component

Julie
Julidochromis ornatus

One feature of the cichlids from the lakes of the African Rift Valley is the way in which several different species, occurring in separate localities, have evolved a similar appearance. The body shape and pattern of coloration of the julie is similar to that of the female Malawi golden cichlid (see page 112). However, you cannot determine the sex of the julie by its coloration or patterning. These differences reflect variations in local populations. Julies from northern parts of their range have more intensive yellow underparts, for example, compared with those from the southern area of the lake. Keep pairs on their own, and they will form a strong pair bond.

The best way of identifying true pairs is based on the size of the julies—mature males are slightly smaller than females when fully grown.

Julies are cave breeders, with females laying only small clutches of approximately 30 eggs. A clay flowerpot will be a good breeding site in a tank. The young will hatch in three days, but they cluster together on the walls of the cave for five days, until they are free-swimming.

data box

FAMILY: **Cichlidae**
SIZE: **5 inches (12.5cm)**
WATER CONDITIONS: **Hard and alkaline**
DISTRIBUTION: **Lake Tanganyika in East Africa**
HABITAT: **Relatively shallow water**
COMPATIBILITY: **Males are aggressive**
DIET: **Prepared cichlid food plus live foods**

White-spotted cichlid
Tropheus duboisi

The spotted pattern of these cichlids is only seen in juveniles, fading as the fish mature. In common with a number of other Rift Valley cichlids, the adults themselves are variable in appearance. Those from the vicinity of the Malagarasi estuary have a wide yellow band around their bodies, while those from other areas have a white band.

White-spotted cichlids are similar in their behavior and requirements to the mbuna cichlids occurring in Lake Malawi, browsing on algae growing on rockwork close to the shore. The males, which have longer pelvic fins than the females, are aggressive toward each other. Keep them individually alongside several females.

After spawning, a female will incubate the eggs in her mouth. These cichlids are not prolific fish, and a female typically produces a maximum of 15 eggs, which are often laid among the rockwork, which should be prominent in their tank. The eggs are

retrieved by the female and incubated in her mouth for about a month, when the young will be large enough to feed on brine shrimp nauplii. The female will continue keeping a watchful eye on her young for a further week, allowing them to dart back inside her mouth if danger threatens.

data box

FAMILY: **Cichlidae**
SIZE: **4½ inches (12cm)**
WATER CONDITIONS: **Hard and alkaline**
DISTRIBUTION: **Lake Tanganyika in East Africa**
HABITAT: **Relatively shallow water**
COMPATIBILITY: **Males are aggressive**
DIET: **Prepared cichlid food plus vegetable matter**

The juvenile fish start off with a black coloration completely covered with white spots.

Malawi butterfly peacock
Aulonocara jacobfreibergi

Although there are a number of different regional color morphs of the Malawi butterfly peacock, rich blue markings predominate on their bodies. Signs of yellow coloration are often most evident in males, and their dorsal and ventral fins are longer than in females, tapering to more clearly defined points. You can keep a single male safely in the company of several females.

Malawi butterfly peacock cichlids will often dig in the substrate, so provide protection for the roots of plants growing in the aquarium to prevent them from being uprooted. These cichlids prefer to feed on worms and similar edible items rather than greenstuff.

Unusually, the male Malawi butterfly peacock can grow significantly larger in an aquarium surrounding than in its natural habitat.

If you want to encourage these cichlids to breed, incorporate a suitable cave area, where the male can display and spawning can take place out of sight. The female will collect the eggs in her mouth, and although the male has no so-called yellow egg spots on his ventral fin to attract her, she will still be drawn to this part of his body. When the male releases sperm, it passes into the female's mouth and fertilizes the eggs.

data box

FAMILY: **Cichlidae**
SIZE: **6inches (15cm)**
WATER CONDITIONS: **Hard and alkaline**
DISTRIBUTION: **Lake Malawi in East Africa**
HABITAT: **Rocky, relatively shallow water**
COMPATIBILITY: **Males are aggressive**
DIET: **Prepared cichlid foods and live foods**

Brevis

Neolamprologus brevis

Compared with some of the other cichlids found in Rift Valley waters, brevis are small and relatively dull in color, being mainly fawn brown.

The common names given to many Rift Valley cichlids are often derived from their scientific names, as in this case. The breeding behavior of brevis is fascinating. These cichlids inhabit parts of the lake where snails are abundant. However, brevis do not feed on these molluscs but use their empty shells for breeding purposes.

Design an aquarium for a pair of these cichlids with a sandy base, and incorporate several empty shells of large edible snails (*Helix* species), which are often available through gourmet food stores. Females, which can be identified by their much smaller size and lack of an orange border around the dorsal and caudal fins, will occupy these shells, both as retreats from danger and as spawning sites.

These egg-laying cichlids only produce small clutches, which are likely to be comprised of fewer than 20 eggs. The larger male does not enter the shell itself, but simply fertilizes them from outside, with his milt being carried inside the shell by the water. The female then guards the eggs, with the young emerging from the shell once they are a week old.

data box

FAMILY: Cichlidae
SIZE: Up to 2 inches (5cm)
WATER CONDITIONS: Hard and alkaline
DISTRIBUTION: Lake Tanganyika in East Africa
HABITAT: Sandy areas through the lake
COMPATIBILITY: Julies (see page 114) are suitable companions
DIET: Small prepared cichlid foods and live foods

Labidochromis electric yellow
Labidochromis caeruleus

There is tremendous variation in the color of these cichlids, which occur in different localities around Lake Malawi. The most brightly colored yellow specimens originate from the vicinity of Kakusa, whereas the darkest deep blue examples are found in Nkhata Bay. These different morphs may be sold under various names, depending on their coloration.

Although labidochromis is a mbuna cichlid, it has a placid disposition. This has helped its popularity among fish keepers, who can keep it in the company of other nonaggressive cichlids that require similar aquarium conditions. Even so, you should keep a male, recognizable by his black ventral fins, with several females.

All labidochromis electric yellow have a black stripe extending along the dorsal fin, which extends down the center of the back.

Incorporate suitable retreats in an aquarium for labidochromis so that the females can use them for spawning. This species is a typical mouthbreeder, with a female not feeding for three weeks or so afterward, until the young have hatched and leave the relative safety of her mouth.

data box

FAMILY: Cichlidae
SIZE: Up to 6 inches (15cm)
WATER CONDITIONS: Hard and alkaline
DISTRIBUTION: Lake Malawi in East Africa
HABITAT: Rocky areas close to the shoreline
COMPATIBILITY: Relatively tolerant in a spacious aquarium
DIET: Prepared cichlid food, greenstuff, and live foods

Kribensis

Pelvicachromis pulcher

Young kribensis can be sexed when five months old. The female is smaller in size than the male and has a more vibrant color.

These attractive African cichlids are easily sexed, because the female has a more vibrant purplish-red area on the belly, which explains their alternative name of purple krib. Kribensis are often found in slightly brackish waters, so the addition of a little marine salt to their aquarium water is often recommended, although not essential.

A pair of kribensis should thrive in a well-planted aquarium in which a flowerpot or a similar cavelike structure has been incorporated, which the female can adopt as a spawning site in due course. Raising the water temperature in the aquarium by a degree or so Fahrenheit can help to trigger breeding behavior, as will increasing the amount of live foods in their diet.

These cichlids may prey on their early broods, but this phase will pass once the pair are more settled in their quarters. The female will lay up to 100 eggs at a time. The fry are free-swimming about five days after hatching, and at this time they can be reared successfully on brine shrimp nauplii and powdered flake food. The adult pair will usually look after their offspring for up to six weeks.

data box

FAMILY: **Cichlidae**
SIZE: **5¼ inches (13cm)**
WATER CONDITIONS: **Soft and neutral**
DISTRIBUTION: **Coastal region of Nigeria, West Africa**
HABITAT: **Streams and slow-flowing rivers**
COMPATIBILITY: **Territorial when breeding**
DIET: **Prepared cichlid food, greenstuff, and live foods**

Killifish

The slender, small and often vividly colored killifish are one of the most fascinating groups of all aquarium fish, although they are not widely available through most aquatic stores. They are usually kept by groups of enthusiasts.

The colorful killifish

The patterning on killifish varies even between members of the same species, because populations have developed in isolation. Many of the African killifish have an annual life cycle, while those from Asia and the Americas spawn among plants.

The breeding cycle of the "annual killifish" reflects their habitat of pools. These fish mature rapidly, as the water level in the pool evaporates, so they spawn in the mud at the base. The adult fish die, but the eggs remain in the mud until the rains return, when they hatch. Not all eggs hatch immediately, and some fry may not emerge until the following year. When breeding killifish in aquaria, expose the substrate in which the eggs are laid to water at least twice.

must know

▶ Join a killifish society to obtain annual killifish eggs from breeders. You will have to hatch them.
▶ Annual species need soft and acidic waters, representing the rain-filled pools in which they occur naturally.
▶ Many killifish require live foods, so set up live cultures to ensure that suitable food is available.

To help maintain the distinctive appearances found on killifish, such as Günther's nothobranch (*Nothobranchius guentheri*), try to keep the different populations of killifish pure when pairing the fish.

Lyretail
Aphyosemion australe

These killifish are so-called thanks to the shape of the projections on the top and bottom of the caudal fin of the male. An aquarium for lyretail killifish does not need to be especially large, but it must be covered to prevent these lively fish from jumping out of the tank. You can keep a single male with two or three females. Alternatively, if space permits, you can house a larger group of four or five males in the company of a dozen females. This lessens the likelihood of one male being picked upon and bullied, as will happen if just two males are present together. Avoid mixing lyretails with other killifish, because they may hybridize.

The male lyretail is more colorful than the female, who has a caudal fin that is more rounded in shape than the male's caudal fin.

The lyretail lives in permanent stretches of water in the wild, so they do not spawn on the substrate but among aquarium plants, such as Java moss *(Vesicularia dubyana)*. Keep the water level in the tank relatively low, and include floating plants at the surface to make these fish less nervous.

data box

FAMILY: **Aplocheilidae**
SIZE: **2⅓ inches (6cm)**
WATER CONDITIONS: **Soft and acidic**
DISTRIBUTION: **West Africa, in Gabon, Cameroon, and Zaire**
HABITAT: **Rainforest pools**
COMPATIBILITY: **Reasonably social together**
DIET: **Prepared foods and small live foods**

Clown killifish
Pseudepiplatys annulatus

The clown killifish has a distinctive banded pattern, which is unusual in this group of fish. The fins of the males are more brightly colored than those of the females, with red markings clearly apparent in the caudal fin. The males can also be distinguished by their blue irises.

As with other killifish, you should keep these fish in a group on their own. They will also benefit from having a substrate consisting of aquarium peat. This will help to maintain suitable water conditions, as well as mimic the darkened surroundings of their natural environment.

Clown killifish usually spend much of their time close to the water surface and often hide there under floating plants. Spawning will also take place in this part of the aquarium, with the eggs sometimes being laid in clumps of fine-leaved plants.

The clown killifish can be identified by the alternating black and light sections that encircle its body.

Alternatively, provide a spawning mop for the fish to lay eggs.

The young fish will hatch after eight days or so, but it is best to confine them in a relatively small volume of water at first. This is because these killifish tend not to hunt tiny aquatic creatures actively—instead, they are ambush predators, grabbing prey as it swims past. In larger volumes of water, they are at risk of starvation if their food is not within easy reach.

data box

FAMILY: Aplocheilidae
SIZE: 2 inches (5cm)
WATER CONDITIONS: Soft and acidic
DISTRIBUTION: West Africa, in Sierra Leone, Liberia, and Guinea
HABITAT: Rainforest pools
COMPATIBILITY: Reasonably social together
DIET: Prepared foods and small live foods

Günther's nothobranch

Nothobranchus guentheri

Günther's nothobranch is one of the most colorful of the so-called annual killifish.

Different populations of nothobranchius killifish can vary quite widely in coloration, because they are frequently isolated in temporary areas of water within their range. The males are aggressive, so keep a single male with several females in a tank, which should have a substrate of aquarium peat. These fish require relatively few plants; however, they will need plenty of open space for swimming.

You can usually induce spawning by lowering the water level and increasing the water temperature. These adjustments will mimic the conditions that occur in the fish's natural habitat, in which the pools begin to dry up. The females will deposit their eggs in the substrate. Remove the fish after they spawn, allow the water to evaporate until the peat is just damp and then place it, and the eggs, in a plastic bag.

After three months, tip the peat back into a tank and flood it with mature tank water. This should trigger the hatching of the young killifish within a month, just as happens when the rains return in the wild.

The fry will require a fry food or infusoria at first, and they grow quickly. They will themselves be able to breed by the time they are three months old.

data box

FAMILY: **Aplocheilidae**
SIZE: **2 inches (5cm)**
WATER CONDITIONS: **Soft and acidic**
DISTRIBUTION: **Island of Zanzibar off the coast of East Africa**
HABITAT: **Temporary pools**
COMPATIBILITY: **Males are quarrelsome**
DIET: **Prepared foods and small live foods**

American flagfish
Jordanella floridae

The American flagfish is a relatively hardy species and it is possible to keep them in an aquarium without additional heating, providing the water temperature does not fall below 66°F (19°C). House them in a large, well-planted aquarium, with retreats to help restrict territorial disputes between males. In small aquaria, it will be better to house a single male with two females.

Keep the tank well lit to encourage the development of algae on the rockwork and elsewhere, which will be eagerly eaten by American flagfish. As the time for breeding approaches, often triggered by a rise in water temperature, a pair will start to dig a spawning pit in the substrate, where they

will deposit about 70 eggs. However, sometimes the eggs are scattered through plants in the aquarium. Remove the female after spawning, but leave the male to guard the eggs. Once the fry hatch, about a week later, remove the male, too.

Males are more brightly colored than females, with prominent yellow and reddish-brown coloring on their bodies, whereas females have blackish markings.

data box

FAMILY: **Cyprinodontidae**
SIZE: **2½ inches (6.5cm)**
WATER CONDITIONS: **Relatively hard and neutral**
DISTRIBUTION: **Centered on the Florida peninsula**
HABITAT: **Lakes as well as other well-vegetated waters**
COMPATIBILITY: **Males are quarrelsome**
DIET: **Prepared foods, greenstuff, and live foods**

Poecilids

Members of this group include long-time aquarium favorites such as guppies, mollies, platies, and swordtails. These fish have become popular with generations of aquarists simply because they are attractive, easy to keep, and ideal for a community tank.

Live-bearing poecilids

The most popular poecilids are bred in huge numbers and are far removed from their wild relatives, but breeders also work with rarer species, offering a great scope. Because these fish are small in size, they are easy to keep in the aquarium.

The chances of successful breeding are relatively high, because these fish are all live-bearers, which means that instead of laying eggs, like most aquarium fish, they give birth to live young. Provided that you keep the fry out of reach of adult fish, they are much easier to rear than the young of egg-laying species, thanks in part to the fry's larger size. You can even feed them tiny pieces of flaked food, crumbled through the fingers to form a powder.

must know

▶ Before buying poecilids, check all fish in the tank for white spot (see page 175)—it is common on live-bearers.
▶ Some male live-bearers are aggressive toward others of their own kind.
▶ Live-bearers tend to live in the upper part of the aquarium, so keep it covered to prevent them from jumping out.

Greenstuff plays an important part in the diets of many live-bearers, including the molly *(Poecilia velifera)*, so allow some algae to develop in the aquarium. There are also special diets available for certain live-bearers.

Guppy
Poecilia reticulata

Guppies rank among the most popular tropical fish in the world today. This is partly because they are easy to look after and can be bred without difficulty, which means they appeal to those who have little previous experience of fish keeping.

These fish have been developed in a striking array of colors and patterns, far removed from their wild ancestors. There are now special classes for these different varieties of guppies at fish shows, where they are judged competitively on the basis of their appearance. They also have a strong appeal to more experienced fish keepers, who are keen to develop exhibition strains for this purpose.

Without looking for the gonopodium, guppies are still easily sexed—the females are larger in size and less colorful than the males.

A group of guppies will make an impressive display together, although you can keep them together in the company of other nonaggressive fish as part of a community aquarium. However, do not mix those with elaborate fins with fish, such as barbs, which are likely to be fin nippers.

Aside from the different color varieties, there are a number of guppies with striking patterns, such as the cobra guppy. These and similarly patterned varieties are attractive when they also have an enlarged caudal fin, because this gives a wider area over which this patterning can be displayed. The caudal fin may be a rounded or delta shape, a swordtail with a longer projection, or even a lyretail with projections top and bottom; most swordtail and lyretail guppies have a dorsal fin with a long pointed shape.

This blonde red guppy is one of the many color variations available, which can range from shades of yellow to red, green, and blue.

The green cobra guppy is so-called because of the distinctive snakelike pattern completely covering its body and most of its fins.

Guppies can be sexed without difficulty because, like many live-bearers, the anal fin of the male fish has developed into a rod-like feature, known as the gonopodium. This is used to transfer sperm directly into the female's body during mating.

Guppies are prolific fish, but they have a relatively short lifespan of about a year, so if you purchase adult fish, the likelihood is that they will only live for a few months. Assuming the females give birth, chances are that some of the offspring will not be related to the male fish that you have acquired. This is because female guppies store sperm in their bodies, and can produce many broods in succession

without having to mate. In order to ensure true pairings, breeders separate the sexes as soon as possible, when the young guppies are about three weeks old.

The eggs simply develop within the female's body, without forming a placental attachment of any kind. Unfortunately, as the young emerge, there is a likelihood that they will be eaten, either by their mother, who displays no maternal instincts toward them, or by other fish in the tank. You can add a breeding trap (see page 186) to the tank, which basically keeps the brood safe. Transfer the female to the trap just before she gives birth.

The snakelike pattern is restricted to the caudal fin on this red cobra guppy. The body has the less intense coloration typical of females.

data box

FAMILY: Poeciliidae
SIZE: 2 inches (5cm)
WATER CONDITIONS: Relatively hard and alkaline
DISTRIBUTION: Central and northern South America, and the Caribbean
HABITAT: Ditches to lakes and rivers
COMPATIBILITY: Not aggressive
DIET: Prepared foods, greenstuff, and small live foods

Platy
Xiphophorus maculatus

There are now many different varieties of the platy, based on modifications to the coloration, fin shape, and patterning of these fish. These varieties have arisen in part thanks to natural variations seen within platy populations in the wild, and these have been combined to create the domesticated strains seen today. Platies are sometimes called moonfish because of the presence of a black marking at the base of the caudal fin, which resembles a crescent-shaped moon in appearance.

These live-bearers normally inhabit shallow stretches of water in the wild,

The blue coral platy has a pale whitish-blue form, and it can be identified by the blue spot in front of its crescent-shaped marking on the caudal peduncle.

which warm up quickly when they receive sunlight. Therefore, the platies are often exposed to relatively higher temperatures, so they will appreciate a water temperature of 77°F (25°C) in their quarters. The other effect of the sunlight is to encourage algal growth in these surroundings, so platies will browse on plant matter in the aquarium. You should offer them greenstuff on a regular basis.

Sexing is straightforward on the basis of the size of the fish, with the females growing almost twice as large as males. The females also have an anal fin, lacking the narrow, tubelike gonopodium found on the males, which is used for mating. (Because these fish are live-bearers, fertilization takes place internally.)

The actual extent of the black pigmentation on the black platy is variable. It does not cover the entire body and the face is always pale.

A female will typically produce young about four weeks after mating. In the latter stages, the fact that she is gravid will be evident, as her body swells with the developing eggs. Just prior to giving birth, she is likely to develop what breeders often refer to as the "black spot." This is evident toward the rear of her body, on the flanks. It is caused by the increasing size of her offspring, which force the dark lining of the abdomen against the flank. Not surprisingly, the black spot is most evident in pale-colored platies.

It is not a good idea to catch the female in this state, because this is likely to cause her to abort her brood prematurely. However, if the adult fish are well-fed and not overcrowded, there is a possibility that at least some of the young will survive, particularly if the tank is designed to give them protection. You can achieve this by including plentiful areas of Java moss (*Vesicularia dubyana*) in the aquarium, attached to bogwood, which will provide the fry with adequate retreats until they have grown large enough not to fall prey to the adult fish. They will scavenge tiny food particles, such as pieces of flake food.

As with other live-bearers, female platies may breed almost continuously, even if they are kept on their own, because they can store the male's sperm in their bodies. A female is likely to produce perhaps as many as 80 young on each occasion, although young females will have correspondingly smaller broods.

data box

FAMILY: Poeciliidae
SIZE: 2¼ inches (6cm)
WATER CONDITIONS: Relatively hard and alkaline
DISTRIBUTION: Central America
HABITAT: Standing water, such as pools and marshes
COMPATIBILITY: Not aggressive
DIET: Prepared foods, greenstuff, and small live foods

Swordtail
Xiphophorus helleri

These fish are so-called because of the long, swordlike projection on the lower edge of the caudal fin of the male. This can measure over 3 inches (7.5cm) in some cases. Older females may sometimes develop a swordlike extension on their caudal fin, too, which is thought to be the result of a hormonal imbalance, but they can still be distinguished by their larger size.

Just as with the other popular live-bearers, there are a number of closely related species or subspecies of swordtail, which differ in various respects. Today's popular domestic strains have been bred by combining these different forms to

The coloration of the green swordtail is more reminiscent of wild strains, compared with the vivid orange and yellow shades that are more commonly seen today.

create features such as bright coloration, which can be found on such fish as the pineapple swordtail and the gold swordtail. There are now strains where males have a corresponding extension to the upper tip of their caudal fin.

If you are interested in acquiring the wild-type swordtails with their more subdued coloration, you will have to track them down through speciality breeders. They are uncommon and unlikely to be seen in aquatic stores.

Male swordtails are generally more aggressive by nature than the other commonly kept live-bearers. Although it is feasible to house a male in the company of two or three females, do not do so with another male, as the weaker individual of the two is likely to be bullied relentlessly.

The slightly larger female normally lacks the swordlike projection. The stripe along the sides of the body are reminiscent of the wild strain.

The only way that it is usually possible to keep male swordtails without persistent fighting is to house them in a large tank that can accommodate six to ten specimens. Because they will not come into contact with the same individual so frequently, there is less scope for repeated bullying to occur. Avoid keeping swordtails with barbs and similar companions, which can damage their swordlike extensions. It is also not a good idea to keep swordtails in the company of platies, simply because these live-bearers can actually breed together, producing hybrid offspring.

Swordtails often inhabit fast-flowing water in the wild, so they will benefit from well-oxygenated water. However, you will need to take care if these fish are breeding, because newly born young may find themselves being sucked up into a power filter. In addition, there is little point in trying to breed these fish in a standard aquarium, even if it is well-planted, because the fry are likely to be eaten by the adult fish.

As for all live-bearers, use a breeding tank that has gentle filtration—a sponge filter is ideal. Transfer a gravid female to a breeding trap, and remove her once she has given birth. Rear the young on their own. They tend to grow relatively slowly.

data box

FAMILY: Poeciliidae
SIZE: 4 inches (10cm)
WATER CONDITIONS: Relatively hard and alkaline
DISTRIBUTION: The eastern side of Central America
HABITAT: Fast-flowing waters, with plenty of vegetation
COMPATIBILITY: Males can be extremely quarrelsome
DIET: Prepared foods and small live foods

Molly
Poecilia velifera

Although their precise origins are unknown, there are a number of different mollies, and these have been hybridized to create today's aquarium strains. Nevertheless, there are still signs of differentiation among this species, which can be distinguished by the fish's greatly enlarged dorsal fin—it is often likened to a sail on the top of their bodies.

If you want to keep mollies, you should make sure you house them in an aquarium that contains slightly brackish water. These fish are vulnerable to both fungus and white spot (see pages 175–77) if their surroundings are less than optimal.

Females are larger than males and have a normal anal fin, not the tubelike gonopodium that is characteristic of the males.

Their attractive matte, velvetlike appearance has made black mollies immensely popular. You can create a stunning contrast by housing them in the company of vibrant orange swordtails, which you can also keep in a tank with brackish water.

Color variations include mollies with contrasting silvery and black spotted patterning, as well as marbled individuals. In the case of sailfin mollies, brighter shades have been created, including the so-called marmalade, with its predominantly orange coloration. Lyretailed variants have also been bred in these different colors.

Sailfin mollies have played a role in the development of the balloon molly, which

Black is a color that has become synonymous with mollies, but there are other types, including those with black and silver patterns.

is so-called because of its modified shape, which includes a naturally swollen belly. Lacking the naturally elegant profile of the sailfin itself, the balloon molly can be somewhat cumbersome when swimming. It is important when keeping these two types of molly in an aquarium together that you check there is enough food. Otherwise, the sailfin mollies may take the majority of the food available, usually leaving relatively little for their relatives.

Mollies will also seek natural food in the aquarium, browsing on any algae growing in it. If this greenstuff is in short supply, the mollies will often turn their attentions to aquarium plants. This, combined with the brackish environment, means that only relatively tough plants, such as vallisneria, will thrive in the tank.

Breeding mollies

The breeding habits of mollies are similar to those of swordtails (see pages 130–31). Males may become aggressive toward each other, particularly as they approach breeding time.

Females can give birth to as many as 100 fry in a single brood. The hybrid ancestry of the fish is often highlighted in their offspring as they develop, because some of them develop much smaller and shorter dorsal fins than others. Because mollies generally prefer to swim in the upper part of the aquarium, the young fish often congregate under the trailing roots of floating plants.

data box

FAMILY: **Poeciliidae**
SIZE: **7¼ inches (18cm)**
WATER CONDITIONS: **Relatively hard and alkaline**
DISTRIBUTION: **Originally from Mexico's Yucatán peninsula**
HABITAT: **Brackish waters, with plenty of vegetation**
COMPATIBILITY: **Reasonably social, but males may disagree**
DIET: **Prepared foods, greenstuff, and small live foods**

Western mosquito fish
Gambusia affinis

Mosquito fish gained their name because they will eat the aquatic larval stage in the mosquito's life cycle, helping to prevent the spread of dangerous diseases, such as malaria. They also rely on algae to form a significant component of their diet. These fish are adaptable in terms of the water temperature that they require, largely because in their natural habitat, it often falls significantly during the winter.

Their breeding habits are similar to those of other live-bearers, and females produce broods of 60 or more fry at a time. When a group of western mosquito fish are housed together, the females will give birth every five weeks or so. However, they are highly predatory by nature and there is a risk they will eat their young, even if the adult fish

These live-bearers can be sexed by a difference in size between the sexes—the females grow significantly larger than males.

are well fed. As a precaution, ensure that the aquarium incorporates retreats by using plants such as Java moss (*Vesicularia dubyana*), which allow the young to hide. You can transfer them to a separate tank so they can be reared separately, in safety.

data box

FAMILY: **Poeciliidae**
SIZE: **Males can grow to 1¼ inches (4cm); females can reach 2¾ inches (7cm)**
WATER CONDITIONS: **Relatively hard and neutral**
DISTRIBUTION: **Southeastern USA to northern Vera Cruz, Mexico.**
HABITAT: **Calm stretches of water**
COMPATIBILITY: **Can be kept together in groups**
DIET: **Prepared foods, greenstuff, and small live foods.**

Butterfly goodeid
Ameca splendens

This live-bearer is also known as the ameca. Aquarium strains are well-established. Sexing is straightforward, because apart from a difference in size between the sexes, the female has more prominent black speckling on her body.

Male butterfly goodeids have a yellowish tip to their caudal fin and also a taller dorsal fin. They do not have a gonopodium, but they have a notch in the anal fin called the spermatopodium. This ensures that the eggs are fertilized in the female's body. A male butterfly goodeid is aggressive toward males of his own species, so do not mix them together—otherwise, they are unlikely to disturb other fish in the tank.

Butterfly goodeids breed readily, and the young fish are born with signs of placental-like cords. A female giving birth for the first time will produce a small brood of about 15 offspring after eight weeks gestation. Mature female butterfly goodeids may have double this number of fry. The young vary in size. Unlike some live-bearers, goodeids cannot store sperm, so they need to mate before each brood.

Although butterfly goodeids will eat a wide variety of food, greenstuff is an important component in their diet.

> **data box**
>
> **FAMILY:** Goodeidae
> **SIZE:** 2¼ inches (6cm)
> **WATER CONDITIONS:** Relatively hard and alkaline
> **DISTRIBUTION:** Ameca River in Mexico
> **HABITAT:** Shallow, well-vegetated stretches of fresh water
> **COMPATIBILITY:** Males are quarrelsome
> **DIET:** Prepared foods, greenstuff, and small live foods.

Cyprinids

The cyprinids represent the largest group of all freshwater fish and contain many popular species such as danios, barbs, and rasboras. The goldfish is not just the the most widely kept cyprinid—it is also the most popular pet fish in the world.

The active cyprinids

Cyprinids are active, shoaling fish. In most cases, you should keep them in groups, but there are exceptions, as in the case of the red-tailed black shark (see page 142), which is aggressive toward its own kind. Not all cyprinids need heated surroundings, but many need water that has been filtered through aquarium peat.

The most popular cyprinids are bred commercially on a huge scale, which has led to many color and fin variants. However, breeding these fish in the home aquarium is challenging because they often eat their eggs. You will need to set up a spawning tank, and the fry require special foods until they can feed on food offered to the adult fish, such as powdered flake.

must know

▶ **Sexing cyprinids is difficult, so buy a group of these fish to acquire a breeding pair. Set up a second tank for spawning and rearing fry.**
▶ **Good filtration is essential in a tank for larger cyprinids because they create a large amount of waste. These fish will also need a spacious aquarium on account of their size.**

Barbs, notably the tiger barb *(Barbus tetrazona)*, can be aggressive, and they are likely to nip long, trailing fins of slower swimming fish, so choose tank mates with care. Avoid Siamese fighting fish *(Betta splendens)* if you want to keep tiger barbs.

White Cloud Mountain minnow
Tanichthys albonubes

This attractive fish is a cyprinid that will thrive in an aquarium at room temperature. However, it needs good water circulation and frequent partial water changes to reflect the conditions in its natural habitat. White Cloud Mountain minnows are named after the area of China where they were first discovered in fast-flowing streams.

These fish will look best in a group. You should buy them together instead of from different sources, otherwise they may be reluctant to integrate into a shoal. There are two different color variants, plus a long-finned strain. Adult females tend to be slightly smaller than males.

Raising the water temperature slightly to 72°F (22°C) can trigger spawning, which takes place among fine-leaved aquatic plants such as milfoil *(Myriophyllum)*. If the adult fish are fed well, they are unlikely to eat their eggs or fry, so you can leave the eggs in the tank. Hatching takes about two days, and the young will thrive if offered a fry food and powdered flake at first.

White Cloud Mountain minnows originating from Hong Kong display red edging to their fins—others have a yellow edging.

> **data box**
>
> FAMILY: **Cyprinidae**
> SIZE: **1¼ inches (4cm)**
> WATER CONDITIONS: **Relatively soft and acidic, but adaptable**
> DISTRIBUTION: **Area of Canton, China**
> HABITAT: **Fast-flowing, cool mountain streams**
> COMPATIBILITY: **Lives in groups**
> DIET: **Prepared foods, greenstuff, and live foods**

Goldfish

Carassius auratus

The goldfish is one of the easiest fish to keep in aquarium surroundings, and it can be remarkably long-lived—in exceptional circumstances the life expectancy can be as long as 40 years. There are many different types of goldfish, differing not just in their coloration but also in their physical appearance. However, they are all descended from a fish with a greenish coloration, found in the waterways of southern China. It was here about a thousand years ago that a fisherman noticed off-colored individuals, which

The traditional slim-bodied goldfish, with its orange coloration, was bred from a greenish colored fish with areas of orange on its body.

had scattered orange areas on their bodies. Some of these fish were kept and bred, laying the basis for the development of the goldfish of today.

Goldfish were first taken from China to Japan in about 1500, before finding their way to Europe in the 1700s. Goldfish were introduced to the USA in the late 1800s. Although many popular goldfish varieties were developed hundreds of years ago, until relatively recently, many remained localized to their area of development. This applies to the pearlscale goldfish, for example, which has characteristic pearl-like markings on the flanks of its body and a double caudal fin.

The traditional goldfish is a fish with a relatively slim body and very compact fins, which include a powerful caudal fin. They tend to be orange-red in colour, but as their name suggests, they can also be a variable golden shade. Bicolored orange and white goldfish, which display a highly individual patterning, are very common. Pure white goldfish are also seen occasionally.

Another popular group of goldfish, which is equally suitable for either a pond or an aquarium, are the shubunkins. These have a typically mottled appearance, with a variable depth of blue coloration on their bodies, ranging from light blue to a violet shade, depending on the individual. Orange and whitish markings are also sometimes apparent. There are three different varieties of shubunkin that are recognized for show purposes, and these are named after their

The lionhead goldfish is one of the so-called "fancy" breeds. You can recognize a lionhead by the lack of a dorsal fin on its back and the swelling on the head of a mature fish.

areas of origin—the London, Bristol, and American. These divisions are based primarily on the shape of the caudal fin. However, the difference in the shapes is less apparent in ordinary pet-store stock.

You can recognize the so-called "fancy" breeds of goldfish by their shorter, more compact body shape. This group includes the lionhead and the oranda, both of which develop a swelling known as a hood, or wen, on their head as they mature. These two breeds can be easily distinguished from each other, because the lionhead lacks a dorsal fin in the center of its back. Both can be brightly colored, but darker varieties also exist, including a steely-blue and a chocolate form of the oranda.

One interesting variety of goldfish is the red-capped oranda. This fish holds its dorsal fin up high and has free-flowing double anal and double caudal fins.

One of the most striking varieties of the oranda is the red-capped oranda, with its red hood offset against its white body.

The darkest colored goldfish is the moor, which is blackish with lighter underparts. The eyes of some moors protrude—these fish eyes are described as telescopic-eyed. The breed of goldfish known as the celestial has a dramatic modification of the eyes. They are positioned to look permanently upward, with fleshy growths on the sides of the eyes. Bubble eyes have an even more distinctive appearance, with large sacs under their eyes. These goldfish need a clear area of water in the aquarium, without rocks that could puncture the sacs.

Goldfish are easy to keep in the home aquarium, especially because they do not need heated surroundings. Nevertheless, it will pay to start off with a large aquarium, because these fish can grow fast, although they generally do not become as large in the confines of a tank as in a pond. The tank will need an efficient filtration system to keep the water clean. An undergravel filter is recommended, but it is also worthwhile incorporating a power filter, especially as the fish become larger.

In true carp fashion, goldfish will often dig in the base of the tank, so plant only hardy plants, such as Canadian pondweed (*Elodea canadensis*). Make sure they are well-supported if you do not want them to be constantly uprooted. Feeding is straightforward, and you can easily tame goldfish to come up and feed from your

This young bubble-eye goldfish has fluid-filled swellings under its eyes—ideally, these should be balanced in size.

stand of aquarium plants, although the eggs are often scattered widely around the tank. Goldfish will eat their own eggs, so you will need to move them to another tank.

When the fry hatch after several days, they will remain immobile at first, digesting the remains of their yolk sacs. They will then become free-swimming and require a fry food, but you can also offer them finely powdered flake.

Regular water changes are essential for young fish, and divide them into smaller groups as they grow larger. Growth and color foods for young goldfish are available from most suppliers. All young goldfish are dark in color at first, and it will be at least three months before they start to acquire their distinctive coloration. Some goldfish may not obtain their adult coloration until they are two years old.

hand, using either flake or pelleted foods. Special diets are now available for some of the fancy varieties such as the oranda.

It is difficult to sex goldfish reliably outside the spawning period, although when viewed from above, females may have broader and longer bodies. As the time for spawning approaches, males will develop white pimples on their gill plates, behind the eyes, which extend along the top of the adjacent pectoral fins. There is usually considerable disturbance within the aquarium as the males chase after the females. Spawning usually occurs among a

Each scale on the pearlscale goldfish has a white or pearly colored raised center. The main coloration can vary.

data box

FAMILY: **Cyprinidae**
SIZE: **10 inches (25cm) or more**
WATER CONDITIONS: **Relatively soft and acidic, but adaptable**
DISTRIBUTION: **Southern China**
HABITAT: **Sluggish rivers**
COMPATIBILITY: **Gets along well with other fish**
DIET: **Prepared foods, greenstuff, and live foods**

Red-tailed black shark
Epalzeorhynchos bicolor

The shape of this cyprinid and its red forked tail explains its common name, although it is not related to sharks. The red-tailed black shark is a popular choice for a community aquarium, but it must be kept apart from others of its own kind, including related species, because it is highly territorial by nature. A suitable environment for these fish must include adequate retreats, with a soft, sandy base making the most suitable substrate. The tank should also be quite well-planted, providing good cover.

In an established aquarium, these fish will browse on algae, in addition to taking other food, which should include some greenstuff, such as lettuce. The antisocial nature of the red-tailed black shark means that breeding them in typical aquarium surroundings is not possible. However, they have been spawned successfully in larger setups designed specifically to accommodate a breeding pair. You can distinguish the sexes only when the female swells with eggs.

When young, red-tailed black sharks are actually silvery brown in color at first and do not develop their characteristic red tail until they are about seven weeks old. Their coloration then darkens progressively from brown to black as they mature.

data box

FAMILY: Cyprinidae
SIZE: 6 inches (15cm)
WATER CONDITIONS: Relatively soft and acidic
DISTRIBUTION: Thailand in south-east Asia
HABITAT: Rivers
COMPATIBILITY: Does not get along with its own kind
DIET: Prepared foods including flake, plus fresh greenstuff

The red-tailed black shark has a high dorsal fin and the streamlined body shape reminiscent of sharks.

Mosquito rasbora

Boraras brigittae

Males are usually more brightly colored, so sexing mosquito rasbora is normally relatively straightforward.

These tiny rasboras are easy to manage and will thrive if you keep them together in a shoal. You can also mix them alongside other nonaggressive companions. Their small size makes them an ideal choice for a small aquarium. These rasbora prefer relatively shaded conditions, complete with floating plants at the water surface.

As one of the smallest members of the cyprinid family, this species, like the better-known dwarf rasbora, produces only a small number of eggs at a single spawning, frequently less than 50 in total. Therefore, it is important to try to protect the eggs from the adult fish. Using marbles on the base of the tank can help to safeguard eggs, which fall down through the aquatic vegetation. Before you transfer the fish to the spawning tank, ensure that they are fed well, so they will be less inclined to search

for food. Live foods, such as brine shrimp nauplii, will make an excellent conditioning food for these fish.

The young fish are small when they hatch. Initially, they will require rotifers, a microscopic form of live foods, before you can offer them the same food as adults.

data box

FAMILY: Cyprinidae
SIZE: 1¼ inches (3.5cm)
WATER CONDITIONS: Relatively soft and acidic
DISTRIBUTION: Parts of Indonesia and southern Borneo
HABITAT: Small pools, slow-flowing streams
COMPATIBILITY: Lives in groups
DIET: Prepared foods and live foods

Harlequin rasbora
Trigonostigma heteromorpha

The harlequin is one of the most popular of the rasboras, displaying a characteristic triangular-shaped marking on its flanks. These fish, like other members of the group, require water filtered through aquarium peat to help acidify the water. Arrange the tank with well-planted areas, as well as open spaces where the fish can congregate. The aquarium should have subdued lighting, which you can achieve by incorporating some floating plants.

You should keep these rasboras in shoals. Females have a broader profile when viewed from the side, compared with males. Unfortunately, harlequin rasboras are not especially easy fish to spawn successfully in the home aquarium.

The true harlequin rasbora has a silvery hue to its body. The similar subspecies espes (*R. h. espei*) has an orange hue that is most prominent toward the back of its body.

You will need to set up a separate breeding tank, paying particular attention to the water conditions. Plant cryptocornes in the tank, which are often favored for egg-laying purposes—the eggs will be deposited on the leaves. Transfer the adult fish back to the main aquarium after spawning takes place.

data box

FAMILY: **Cyprinidae**
SIZE: **2 inches (5cm)**
WATER CONDITIONS: **Relatively soft and acidic**
DISTRIBUTION: **Parts of Thailand, Malaysia, and Sumatra**
HABITAT: **Slow-flowing, often shady streams**
COMPATIBILITY: **Strong shoaling instincts**
DIET: **Prepared foods and live foods**

Scissortail rasbora

Rasbora trilineata

The deep caudal fin of the scissortail rasbora gives it its common name. As it swims forwards, the gap between the lobes of its tail close slightly like the blades of a scissor. The species is also called the three-lined rasbora, thanks to the pattern of dark stripes along the sides of its body. The most prominent stripe is at the midline, but there are other stripes along the top of the body and the underparts. This rasbora can swim fast, due to its streamlined shape, so make sure the tank has open areas for swimming purposes.

Sexing scissortail rasboras is difficult, but females may have a more rounded body than males. Spawning occurs in the open, with the eggs simply falling to the substrate, where they are at risk of being consumed by the fish. A covering of marbles on the floor of the spawning tank will give some protection to the eggs until the adult fish can be moved to the main aquarium. This is important, because unlike some cyprinids, spawning normally occurs overnight instead of first thing in the morning.

The scissorlike movement of the caudal fin is emphasized by the dark tips on the upper and lower parts of the tail.

data box

FAMILY: **Cyprinidae**
SIZE: **4 inches (10cm)**
WATER CONDITIONS: **Relatively soft and acidic**
DISTRIBUTION: **Parts of Thailand, Malaysia, Sumatra, and Borneo**
HABITAT: **Slow-flowing, often shady streams**
COMPATIBILITY: **Strong shoaling instincts**
DIET: **Prepared food and live foods**

Zebra danio

Danio rerio

The alternating blue and light yellowish stripes of zebra danios suggest their common name. These danios are easy to maintain and look attractive in a shoal, and they tend to swim near the surface of the aquarium. Keep the aquarium covered at all times to prevent the fish from leaping out of the tank.

These danios are not always easy to spawn successfully. Increasing the amount of live foods, such as whiteworm or daphnia, in the diet can help to trigger breeding behavior, when the male fish chase the females into well-planted areas of the tank.

Set up a special breeding tank with fine-leafed plants, such as milfoil *(Myriophyllum)*. The vegetation will provide cover for the female prior to spawning, allowing her to

Both sexes have two pairs of tiny barbels adjacent to the mouth. Females are slightly larger than males, with a more rounded body.

escape the attentions of male fish. It will also serve as somewhere for the female to deposit her eggs in due course.

Egg laying normally occurs in the morning. It is especially important to remove the adult danios as soon as possible afterward, because they will consume their spawn. Hatching will take about two days after spawning.

data box

FAMILY: **Cyprinidae**
SIZE: **2 inches (5cm)**
WATER CONDITIONS: **Relatively soft and acidic**
DISTRIBUTION: **Parts of Bangladesh and eastern India**
HABITAT: **Slow-flowing stretches of water**
COMPATIBILITY: **Strong shoaling instincts**
DIET: **Prepared foods and live foods**

Great danio

Devario aequipinnatus

The individual markings on great danios enable them to be distinguished from each other.

Although these danios can grow much larger than related species, they can usually be kept without problems in a community aquarium. In common with other danios, they are active by nature and tend to prefer swimming in the upper part of the aquarium. They have yellow stripes and broader blue bands extending along the sides of the silvery-grey body.

It is usually possible to sex great danios on the basis of their shape, with females having broader bodies than males. The central blue stripe in female fish also tends to be slightly upturned at its end, on the caudal fin. Great danios will breed before they attain full size, being mature by the time they are around 2½ inches (6cm) long.

Offering an increased amount of live foods, such as whiteworm, to the adults and raising the water temperature slightly can help to trigger breeding behavior. You should set up a separate tank for breeding purposes, with marbles on the base, to safeguard the eggs—otherwise, the adult fish may eat them. Make sure it is well-stocked with strands of fine-leaved aquatic plants, where spawning can take place.

data box

FAMILY: Cyprinidae
SIZE: 6 inches (15cm)
WATER CONDITIONS: Relatively soft and acidic
DISTRIBUTION: Sri Lanka and western India
HABITAT: Slow-flowing stretches of water
COMPATIBILITY: Strong shoaling instincts
DIET: Prepared foods and live foods

Rosy barb
Barbus conchonius

These barbs are adaptable by nature, and a shoal swimming in open areas will look attractive in an aquarium. There is also a long-finned form of this cyprinid available. These fish will also need a well-planted area in the aquarium. However, they can be rather disruptive fish, particularly if housed with smaller companions, and they also display a tendency to dig in the substrate. Therefore, make sure you weigh down the plants adequately to prevent them from floating to the surface.

Water conditions will need to be optimal to encourage spawning, and setting up a special aquarium for this purpose is usually recommended. Although these barbs can normally thrive under even medium-hard water conditions, they require soft water surroundings when breeding. Rosy barbs are also avid egg eaters, and once a pair have spawned successfully, you will need to transfer them back to the main aquarium without delay to protect their eggs. Spawning itself is likely to take place among

plants, such as Java moss *(Vesicularia dubyana)*, with the fry hatching about a day later. You can offer them a suitable fry food once they become free-swimming, which usually occurs after they digest the remains of their yolk sac.

> **data box**
>
> **FAMILY:** Cyprinidae
> **SIZE:** 5 inches (12.5cm)
> **WATER CONDITIONS:** Relatively soft and neutral
> **DISTRIBUTION:** Northeastern parts of India
> **HABITAT:** Slow-flowing stretches of water
> **COMPATIBILITY:** Strong shoaling instincts
> **DIET:** Prepared foods, greenstuff, and live foods

The reddish coloration of the rosy barb is especially pronounced in males when in spawning condition. Females have a more rotund body shape.

Tiger barb
Barbus tetrazona

These barbs can be more aggressive than related species and cannot be trusted alongside fish that have long, flowing fins in a community tank because they often nibble at their fins. However, such is the popularity of the tiger barb, which has vertical black bands on its body, that there are now several different color variants. They include the red tiger barb, which has an overall reddish coloration and is free of the dark banding. There is also a green variety, sometimes called the moss-banded, thanks to the underlying color of its body. Always check the entire tank of tiger barbs before buying any. They are susceptible to white spot (see page 175).

The striped tiger barb will display the typical shoaling behavior normally associated with this group of fish.

As they spawn, the male twists the rear end of his body around that of the female, fertilizing the eggs as she releases them. These barbs can be prolific when breeding, with a single female producing up to as many as 1,000 eggs at a single spawning.

data box

FAMILY: **Cyprinidae**
SIZE: **2¾ inches (7cm)**
WATER CONDITIONS: **Relatively soft and slightly acidic**
DISTRIBUTION: **Southeast Asia, including Sumatra and Borneo**
HABITAT: **Slow-flowing stretches of water**
COMPATIBILITY: **Strong shoaling instincts**
DIET: **Prepared foods, greenstuff, and live foods**

Tinfoil barb

Barbus schwanefeldi

These barbs will attain a much larger size than the other species available, so they are not suitable for a typical community aquarium. They will rapidly outgrow their companions, and may even prey on them. Nevertheless, tinfoil barbs look spectacular in a large aquarium with nonaggressive species, such as some of the larger catfish, or certain cichlids that require similar water conditions. Keep tinfoil barbs in small shoals instead of individually, because if kept on their own, these fish are nervous and will hide in the aquarium. Young individuals are far less colorful than adults, lacking the dark markings apparent on their fins.

The more common variety of the tinfoil barb has a silver body—however, there is also a golden form that is now available.

Include robust and fast-growing plants in the tank because these cyprinids feed on vegetation and dig in the substrate, leaving them at risk of being uprooted. Setting the plants in small pots may help to prevent them from being disturbed. You can also weigh them down with heavier stones.

data box

FAMILY: **Cyprinidae**
SIZE: **14 inches (35cm)**
WATER CONDITIONS: **Relatively soft and slightly acidic**
DISTRIBUTION: **Southeast Asia**
HABITAT: **Slow-flowing stretches of water**
COMPATIBILITY: **Strong shoaling instincts**
DIET: **Prepared foods, greenstuff, and live food**

Siamese flying fox

Crossocheilus siamensis

Because the Siamese flying fox is territorial by nature, keep only one of these fish in a community aquarium.

In any aquarium, it can be useful to have fish that will browse on the algae, helping to keep it in check. This is particularly true in a newly established setup, where algal growth can to be a particular problem. The Siamese flying fox is an especially useful fish for this purpose because it will even browse on thread algae, which can clog up the leaves of other plants. Another point in its favou is that this cyprinid is likely to restrict its attentions to the algae instead of damaging the plants themselves.

The Siamese flying fox is relatively shy by nature, so there must be well-planted areas in the aquarium that can serve as retreats for the fish. It will spend much of its time close to the base of the tank. You should make sure the aquarium is well oxygenated, because these fish naturally occur in fast-flowing water.

The flying fox *(Epalzeorhynchus kallopterus)* is another fish that is similar in its habits and appearance to the Siamese flying fox, although it is less brightly colored. It will also browse on algae, as well as eat worms and similar live foods. It is equally territorial by nature toward its own kind, so you should keep only one in a tank.

data box

FAMILY: Cyprinidae
SIZE: 6 inches (15cm)
WATER CONDITIONS: Relatively soft and slightly acidic
DISTRIBUTION: Southeast Asia, Thailand, and Malayasia
HABITAT: Streams
COMPATIBILITY: Best to keep apart from its own kind
DIET: Greenstuff and live foods

Miscellaneous

There are many other types of fish, and their appearance often says much about their behavior—from the burrowing wormlike loaches to the flat-backed butterfly fish, which live close to the water's surface. There are also relatively new varieties available.

Establishing new breeds

New varieties occur when an intrepid collector obtains some initial breeding stock, and the offspring of these fish are passed to other experienced fish keepers, allowing their numbers to grow quickly. From here, they will turn up in specialized aquatic outlets, before becoming generally available, depending on their popularity.

By keeping more unusual fish, you have an opportunity to add to existing knowledge about that species. You can record your observations on the breeding attempts of your fish—whether they are ultimately successful or not—and you can post this information on bulletin boards for fellow enthusiasts or write an article for one of the fish-keeping publications.

must know

▶ **Unusual fish may have specialized requirements and may be unsuitable for a community tank. Feeding predatory species that may only eat other fish can present difficulties.**
▶ **Rays have a spine that injects venom into the body if it pierces the skin. They are not suitable for the novice owner.**

The rainbow fish is one group that has grown in popularity in recent years. With any fish, never buy one without knowing what it is—you will not be able to care for it properly and it might outgrow your tank. If the store cannot help you, try researching on the Internet.

Coolie loach
Acanthophthalmus kuhlii

Although strikingly patterned, the coolie loach is not a conspicuous aquarium occupant, being secretive by nature and usually hiding during the day. They will seek hiding places among rockwork and other tank decor, often retreating under a gap between bogwood and the substrate where they will be well-hidden.

Coolie loaches naturally display some variation in their pattern of banding, so sexing them visually is impossible. Even so, successful breeding may occur, if some of their unusual bright green eggs escape being eaten by other tank occupants.

If you need to catch a coolie loach, do so carefully, partly because it will retreat into inaccessible localities, but also because it has small spines beneath each eye, which

Its wormlike shape allows the coolie loach to burrow effectively. It prefers a soft, sandy substrate in the aquarium for this purpose.

can become caught in the fine material of a net. Make sure you free it from a net gently. A less direct alternative is to place a piece of narrow, clean plastic tubing in the tank as a trap, then simply lift it out once the loach retreats inside it, but first place a finger and thumb over the ends.

data box

FAMILY: **Cobitidae**
SIZE: **4 inches (10cm)**
WATER CONDITIONS: **Relatively soft and slightly acidic**
DISTRIBUTION: **Malay Peninsula and parts of Indonesia**
HABITAT: **Slow-flowing, soft-bottomed waters**
COMPATIBILITY: **Social and not aggressive**
DIET: **Food tablets and wormlike live foods**

Clown loach
Botia macracanthus

The brightly coloured clown loach, which is active during the day, is often included when young in a community aquarium. However, it can grow large enough to prey on other, smaller tank occupants. One particular characteristic, which can be alarming when first observed, is the way in which a clown loach rests at a strange angle in the water, with its body tilted on its side. There is no need for concern as this is normal behavior for this fish.

Both sexes have tiny protective spikes just in front of their eyes. The barbels on the underside of the snout help clown loaches to find their food. These fish often dig in the substrate, so you should house them in an aquarium that includes some sandy areas, and make sure you also incorporate bogwood and rockwork to provide retreats.

The depth of coloration may vary, depending on environmental conditions and diet, so a fish's color cannot provide a means of distinguishing

the fish's sex. Instead, it may be possible to identify the male fish by its relatively larger caudal fin. Unfortunately, these loaches are unlikely to breed in the confines of the aquarium surroundings.

> **data box**
>
> **FAMILY: Cobitidae**
> **SIZE: 12 inches (30cm)**
> **WATER CONDITIONS: Relatively soft and slightly acidic**
> **DISTRIBUTION: Indonesia, notably Sumatra, and Borneo**
> **HABITAT: Well-oxygenated, soft-bottomed streams**
> **COMPATIBILITY: Not troublesome when small**
> **DIET: Food tablets and wormlike live foods**

Because of their striped patterning, these fish are also sometimes called tiger loaches.

Polka-dot loach

Botia kubotai

You can keep polka-dot loaches successfully with a wide variety of fish that require similar water conditions. However, they will eat fry and may not agree with other loaches.

This particular species is relatively new and has only been available to fish keepers since about 2002. It is also known as the Burmese border loach and as the angelicus loach. Polka-dot loaches will alter significantly in appearance as they age. Young fish display a range of stripes and bars, with four yellow blotches down their flanks. As they mature, the blackish markings will expand, while the yellowish areas will become more restricted in size. A series of pale spots will start to appear alongside them.

Polka-dot loaches have proved to be highly social, so you should keep them in groups. The aquarium will need a power filter to create a suitable current and to help ensure the water is well oxygenated. Make sure the tank is well planted to provide retreats.

Once the loaches are settled in their aquarium, they will become quite tame, and may sometimes even be persuaded to take food from the hand. These loaches will eat a wide variety of items, ranging from flake and bloodworm to greenstuff, such as peas and zucchini.

data box

FAMILY: Cobitidae
SIZE: 4¾ inches (12cm)
WATER CONDITIONS: Slightly soft and around neutral
DISTRIBUTION: Ataran River Basin in Myanmar (Burma)
HABITAT: Fast-flowing water
COMPATIBILITY: Social and tolerant
DIET: Prepared foods, greenstuff, and live foods

Boeseman's rainbowfish
Melanotaenia boesemani

Rainbowfish as a group have increased in popularity among fish keepers over recent years. Boeseman's rainbowfish, originally discovered by Dr. Marinus Boeseman in 1954, have been bred in aquaria for more than 20 years. They will thrive in a shoal, and the males are easy to distinguish thanks to their brighter coloration, as well as the longer rays on their dorsal fins.

Their aquarium must have plenty of swimming space available, and you will need to keep it covered to ensure the rainbowfish cannot leap out of the tank. These fish are easy to breed successfully, and Java moss *(Vesicularia dubyana)* is a popular choice as a spawning site in their breeding quarters.

Boeseman's rainbowfish are attractive with unusual coloration—and they also have peaceful temperaments.

The eggs will usually take about a week to hatch, and unlike other egg layers, the fry grow relatively slowly, so you will need to offer them infusoria or a similar substitute for nearly a week after they become free-swimming. You will have to wait a year before the young rainbowfish acquire their full adult coloration.

data box

FAMILY: **Melanotaeniidae**
SIZE: **4 inches (10cm)**
WATER CONDITIONS: **Slightly soft and around neutral**
DISTRIBUTION: **Vogelkop peninsula, Irian Jaya, New Guinea**
HABITAT: **Ajamaru Lakes**
COMPATIBILITY: **Social**
DIET: **Prepared foods and live foods**

Lake Kutubu rainbowfish

Melanotaenia lacustris

The bluish coloration is far less apparent in young fish of either sex and is most prominent in mature males.

The beautiful bluish shades on the flanks of the Lake Kutubu rainbowfish vary in their depth of color. Water conditions and the aquarium lighting can also have a significant influence too.

Originating from a highland area, these rainbowfish will require a lower water temperature of 72–77°F (22–25°C). They will also benefit from having a relatively large expanse of open water for swimming purposes, as they would have in the natural environment. Lake Kutubu rainbowfish shoal quite close to the water's surface, so offer them flake food, which floats at the surface. These fish will also eat plant matter, such as duckweed (*Lemna* sp.), which can be easily cultivated in this part of the aquarium. The duckweed will also help to diffuse the level of illumination, which improves the coloration of the fish.

These rainbowfish are relatively easy to breed, with spawning occurring readily in Java moss (*Vesicularia dubyana*). However, the eggs are usually produced in batches over two or three days instead of being laid in rapid succession as occurs among other rainbowfish. The young are relatively large when they hatch, so they will be able to take powdered flake food almost at once.

data box

FAMILY: Melanotaeniidae
SIZE: 4¾ inches (12cm)
WATER CONDITIONS: Hard and alkaline
DISTRIBUTION: Southern highlands of New Guinea
HABITAT: Lake Kutubu and the Soro River
COMPATIBILITY: Social
DIET: Prepared foods and live foods

Red rainbowfish

Glossolepis incisus

The stunning reddish coloration on this rainbowfish is a feature seen only in mature males, who also develop a characteristic dorsal hump. In contrast, females have a slender and elongated appearance and are a yellowish shade, so sexing these rainbowfish when they are adult presents no difficulties.

Red rainbowfish are nervous by nature, so keep them in groups in an aquarium that incorporates a number of hiding places for them among aquatic plants, particularly around the sides and back of the tank. A relatively low water temperature is recommended.

As with other rainbowfish, use a bare spawning tank, with Java moss *(Vesicularia dubyana)* included for egg-laying purposes.

Young males will start to acquire early signs of their characteristic coloration when they are approximately 2 inches (5cm) long.

Spawning itself is protracted and takes place in the morning over the course of several days, with the eggs sticking to the vegetation where they are deposited. The fry should hatch about a week later and will immediately seek food close to the surface. Tiny particles of egg yolk can be a valuable rearing food at this stage, but remember that any left uneaten will cause a rapid deterioration in water quality, so offer this food frequently but in small amounts.

data box

FAMILY: **Melanotaeniidae**
SIZE: **6 inches (15cm)**
WATER CONDITIONS: **Hard and neutral**
DISTRIBUTION: **Northern New Guinea**
HABITAT: **Lake Sentani**
COMPATIBILITY: **Social**
DIET: **Prepared foods and live foods**

Threadfin rainbowfish

Iriatherina werneri

This rainbowfish is so-called thanks to the long, threadlike filaments on the male's second dorsal fin. Unusually, rainbowfish have a dorsal fin that is split into two parts, and they can raise each part independently. The more elaborate rear portion is used in particular by a male, who flicks it up and down when displaying to a mate.

Keep these rainbowfish in groups in a spacious aquarium that provides them with plenty of swimming space. Breeding is not difficult, and small live foods are ideal for conditioning purposes. The females spawn over several days and deposit their eggs in Java moss *(Vesicularia dubyana)*. The young will be small when they hatch about ten days later, and they remain close to the surface. You can feed them small particles of food such as powdered egg yolk. Do not overfeed them—any uneaten food will rapidly pollute the water. As they grow older, give them flake food powdered to dust by being rubbed through clean fingers.

Threadfin rainbowfish descended from New Guinea have redder dorsal fins than those found in Australia.

data box

FAMILY: **Melanotaeniidae**
SIZE: **2 inches (5cm)**
WATER CONDITIONS: **Relatively soft and neutral**
DISTRIBUTION: **New Guinea and northern Australia**
HABITAT: **River drainage systems**
COMPATIBILITY: **Social**
DIET: **Prepared foods and live foods**

Elephant-nosed fish

Gnathonemus petersii

This unusual fish is so-called because of its trunklike proboscis, which it uses to dig in muddy stretches of water to obtain worms. These make up much of its diet, and it can be difficult to persuade the elephant-nosed fish to take substitute foods in aquarium surroundings. The fish will benefit from having a fine, sandy substrate where it can dig for food. Make sure the aquarium is also well planted to provide cover. Some of these fish are playful and will roll a small, clean ball of aluminum foil around the surface of the tank with their mouthparts.

The elephant-nosed fish has a large brain and a highly developed nervous system, including an electrical organ at the base of its caudal peduncle. This produces a series

Before acquiring an elephant-nosed fish, make sure you can supply adequate food because a new fish may only accept worms.

of pulses that help to orientate the fish, especially after dark. Avoid keeping these and related mormyrids together, because these electrical discharges will upset their companions, and they are territorial by nature. However, the elephant-nosed fish is not aggressive toward other fish.

> **data box**
>
> FAMILY: **Mormyridae**
> SIZE: **9 inches (23cm)**
> WATER CONDITIONS: **Relatively soft and acidic**
> DISTRIBUTION: **Western and central Africa**
> HABITAT: **River drainage systems**
> COMPATIBILITY: **Antisocial toward its own kind**
> DIET: **Prefers live foods**

African knifefish
Xenomystus nigri

Similar in some respects to the mormyrid group, the African knifefish is so-called because of its knifelike shape. The anal and caudal fins of the knifefish are fused together, running along the underside of the body to create a wavy appendage that extends to the tip of the tail, with the anal fin itself starting close to the head. Knifefish can gulp down air directly from the atmosphere, rising to the surface of the aquarium for this purpose. They may make unusual sounds, which are the result of air passing out of the swim bladder.

You should set up a tank similar to the one recommended for the elephant-nosed fish (see opposite). The African knifefish tends to become more active toward dusk, and it will prefer a shaded environment, with floating plants at the water's surface to help diffuse the aquarium lighting.

Make sure you house the African knifefish separately from others of its own kind, particularly as it becomes older,

because it will become increasingly territorial. When African knifefish are in breeding condition, their coloration should turn purplish.

data box

FAMILY: **Notopteridae**
SIZE: **8 inches (20cm)**
WATER CONDITIONS: **Relatively soft and acidic**
DISTRIBUTION: **From West Africa, in the Niger River**
HABITAT: **Rivers and associated waterways**
COMPATIBILITY: **Antisocial toward its own kind**
DIET: **Prefers live foods, especially small worms**

This African knifefish has an electrical organ, which allows the fish to orientate itself when swimming after dark or in muddy water.

Butterflyfish
Pantodon buchholzi

The butterflyfish can use the broad shape of their pectoral fins, which resemble those of one of these insects in flight, to propel themselves out of the water. Hence the reason to keep the tank covered as much as possible, even when maintaining the tank.

Butterflyfish do not need a deep tank. They congregate at the surface, so include floating plants in the tank. These fish are ambush predators by nature, hiding under aquatic vegetation and leaping out to grab passing invertebrates. While they will agree well in a small group together, do not keep them with other surface-feeders, such as hatchetfish (see page 95).

Breeding butterflyfish successfully in aquarium surroundings is challenging. If

they do spawn, their eggs will float at the surface. Transfer them to a separate tank, where hatching should take place about three days later. Minute live foods are essential for the fry. You can try springtails *(Collembola)*—these are tiny terrestrial insects, which can be obtained as starter cultures from live-food suppliers.

The butterflyfish can use their broad pectoral fins like wings to glide short distances.

data box

FAMILY: **Pantodontidae**
SIZE: **1¼ inches (4cm)**
WATER CONDITIONS: **Soft, acidic**
DISTRIBUTION: **Eastern Peru, South America**
HABITAT: **Shaded waters**
COMPATIBILITY: **Peaceful, shoaling**
DIET: **Prepared food and live foods**

Indian glassfish
Chanda ranga

Glassfish are so-called because of their transparent bodies. Many species are found in seawater, but some, such as the Indian glassfish, inhabit brackish water. Keep Indian glassfish in a small shoal because this helps to overcome their nervous natures.

When purchasing Indian glassfish, it is especially important to check on the water conditions in which they are being kept, so you will be able to replicate them in your home aquarium. This will help them to acclimatize after the move; then you can make any changes gradually as required. At first, you will need to mix marine salt in with the freshwater, following the instructions given on the packaging to create a solution of the correct strength.

There are some disreputable dealers who have injected glassfish with lurid dyes, which introduces a vivid green or red coloration in their bodies. Do not be tempted to buy any of these fish. Most reputable aquatic stores will refuse to

stock them, because this cruel practice will usually lead to the premature death of the glassfish. In the event that any of these fish do survive, the coloration will soon fade.

data box

FAMILY: **Centropomidae**
SIZE: **3inches (7.5cm)**
WATER CONDITIONS: **Hard and slightly alkaline**
DISTRIBUTION: **Asia, from India east to Thailand**
HABITAT: **Often found in estuaries**
COMPATIBILITY: **Nervous yet peaceful by nature**
DIET: **Prefers live foods; may also eat flaked foods**

The Indian glassfish has a relatively elongated body shape and displays greenish-golden suffusion, depending on the lighting conditions.

Bumblebee goby
Brachygobius xanthozonus

Many gobies are found in the marine environment, where their ventral fins form a suction cup that helps them to anchor onto rocks in turbulent water. However, some species such as the bumblebee goby are found in brackish water.

In view of their size, you can keep these gobies in a relatively small aquarium, but they are best accommodated on their own. Because they are nervous by nature, they are at a disadvantage when obtaining food alongside bolder fish. An aquarium setup for bumblebee gobies will need bogwood and rocks to provide retreats, plus a few plants that thrive in brackish water, such as cryptocornes.

Sexing the bumblebee goby can be difficult, but males are more brightly colored, while females have a stockier profile.

When a pair spawn, the eggs are hidden in a cave or under a rock and are guarded by the male. They are vulnerable to fungus (see pages 174–75), but should hatch after four days. The young occupy the upper part of the tank at first, but move to the base as they become older. You can feed them brine shrimp nauplii when five days of age.

data box

FAMILY: **Gobiidae**
SIZE: **2 inches (5cm)**
WATER CONDITIONS: **Hard and slightly alkaline**
DISTRIBUTION: **Sumatra, Java, and Borneo**
HABITAT: **Often found in estuaries**
COMPATIBILITY: **Territorial and timid**
DIET: **Prepared foods and live foods**

Green pufferfish

Tetraodon fluviatilis

Like other pufferfish, the green pufferfish has four teeth, two on each jaw. If these become overgrown, there is a risk of starvation.

Pufferfish have the ability to inflate their bodies and anchor themselves in a tight space if being attacked. This species requires brackish surroundings, so plastic plants are ideal to create relatively dense cover because most freshwater plants will not grow well in these water conditions. Although young pufferfish will get along well together, they tend to become more aggressive and less tolerant toward others of their kind as they grow older.

It is not a good idea to add aquatic snails in an aquarium accommodating green pufferfish. These fish will prey on the molluscs, crushing them in their strong jaws. Instead, offer pufferfish items such as pieces of shrimp in their shells, which can help to wear down their teeth. If the teeth become overgrown and are not trimmed back, the fish will have difficulty eating.

Sexing these fish by sight is impossible, and breeding them in the home aquarium is difficult because of their aggressive natures. If spawning occurs, it will be close to the substrate with the eggs laid on a rock. The male guards the eggs and watches over his offspring after they hatch by corralling them in a pit dug in the substrate.

data box

FAMILY: **Tetraodontidae**
SIZE: **6 inches (15cm)**
WATER CONDITIONS: **Hard and slightly alkaline**
DISTRIBUTION: **Southeast Asia to the Philippines**
HABITAT: **Often found in estuaries**
COMPATIBILITY: **Somewhat aggressive**
DIET: **Primarily eats live foods**

Caring for your fish

Once your aquarium fish are established in their surroundings, they will be far less likely to fall ill. To give your fish the best chance of staying healthy, feed them a variety of food from the wide range of prepared diets available. Healthy, well-fed fish will often breed successfully in the aquarium, adding another dimension to this fascinating hobby.

1 Keeping your fish healthy

When diseases do strike, they can usually be traced back to environmental problems. Feeding your fish correctly is important because giving them too much food is often the cause of these problems along with poor tank maintenance. Once the aquarium is established, it is still vital to carry out water checks and changes, as well as regular filter maintenance, to ensure optimal conditions for the fish.

Foods and feeding

Most aquarium fish are opportunistic in their feeding habits, so they can be easily persuaded to eat specially formulated foods. Feed your fish a variety of foods, including live foods, to help ensure they stay healthy.

Flaked food is one of the most popular types of dried fish food. It is a convenient way of feeding most fish, especially those that visit the surface of the tank.

Although it may be difficult at first, you'll need to discover roughly how much food your fish will eat. If you feed your fish too much food, it will go uneaten and pollute the water, which can lead to disease. Most fish feed frequently and will benefit from being given food several times each day. However, for nocturnal species, feed them at dusk and again just before you go to bed, when they will be most active. Some feeding guidelines are given on the fish food itself and you can use these as a starting point, but aim to provide no more than the fish will eat within about five minutes of the food being offered.

If you are feeding your fish three or four times during the day, you should vary the food you offer them. For example you can provide a standard dried food, then augment it with a live food of some type. Freeze-dried is the simplest option; alternatively, you can give your fish frozen or live foods (see pages 172–73).

Flakes, pellets, and tablets

The bulk of the diet usually consists of specially

formulated dry foods. These foods are usually inexpensive, especially because the fish eat only relatively small quantities. They need no preparation and are simply used directly from the container. An ever-increasing number of foods are available in aquatic stores, from general-purpose products intended for all the fish in a community aquarium to special diets for particular groups of fish, such as guppies, discus, and goldfish. There are even some that have been designed to help enhance a fish's color.

Large tablets are an option for feeding catfish. For large fish, such as cichlids and goldfish, you can try foodsticks—they are sucked into the fish's mouth lengthwise.

Many prepared dried foods are made in flake form, which has a thin, waferlike appearance. Flaked food will float at the surface of the water for a while, so it is ideal for fish that feed in this area of water. It is also useful for young fish. However, flaked foods tend to be nibbled at, and uneaten food will sink to the gravel, where it can pollute the water.

There are pellets of different types. Pellets are usually eaten whole, which helps to prevent wastage. You should match the size of the fish to that of the pellet. If in doubt, opt for a smaller size of pellet that the fish will be able to swallow easily. Catfish pellets have a denser texture than goldfish pellets and are designed to sink rapidly to the base of the tank, making them ideal for bottom-feeders, such as corydoras. Try to drop these pellets so they fall into a clear area. If they land out of reach, in a crevice between rocks for example, the pellets will pollute the water. Other forms of food suitable for larger fish include tablets and foodsticks.

must know

Prepared dried foods are usually supplemented with the vitamins and minerals that the fish require. Check the expiration date on the packaging, because the quality of the food, especially its vitamin content, will deteriorate after that date. Make sure you store the food in a dry, cool environment.

Supplementary dry foods

A wide range of other prepared dried foods are also available, which can be a useful supplement to a standard diet. They include spirulina, a nutritious form of algae eaten by many fish, which may also help to improve their coloration. Various dried live foods are also available, including daphnia (water fleas) and tubificid worms, as well as river shrimp, which are significantly larger in size and suitable for bigger fish with more predatory feeding habits. In a freeze-dried form, they retain their nutritional value and yet can be stored easily, without having to be refrigerated. They also reduce the risk of introducing disease to the tank. Some foods, such as tubificid worms, are sold as blocks that are dropped into the water—the fish dart up to nibble off pieces.

Frozen foods and live foods

River shrimp are a treat for larger fish. They are available in freeze-dried form, but they are also available as a live food—use these cautiously from a reliable source because they can spread disease.

Store frozen foods, which are usually supplied in small packs, in the freezer and thaw a block just before feeding it to the fish. If you are unlikely to use a whole block, shave off some small sections carefully with a sharp knife. These will thaw quickly at room temperature. Frozen food is usually more palatable than freeze-dried food because it has a higher water content, making it more like natural live foods. Although live foods are available from aquatic stores, they are more likely to introduce disease to the aquarium. Supplies can be unreliable as well, so if you want to offer invertebrates regularly to the fish, the safest option will be to cultivate them yourself.

Other terrestrial live foods, including hatchling crickets (*Gryllus domesticus*) and wingless fruit flies (*Drosophila*), more often sold for reptiles and amphibians, are used to supplement the diets of some fish. However, these are not essential to the well-being of most common aquarium fish.

Certain fish will enjoy a diet supplemented with fresh vegetables. Catfish are fond of zucchini and cucumber, and these also have taken a liking to slices of potato.

Homegrown foods

Some fish keepers prefer to cultivate daphnia in a spare aquarium. Simply remove some with a sieve as required. You can obtain bloodworm, another popular live food, in the summer months by leaving out a bucket of water, where midges can lay their eggs. These hatch into bloodworms, so-called because of their color.

Feeding the vegetarians

As far as the more vegetarian species are concerned, there is no reason why you cannot provide them with fresh items to supplement their regular diet. Slices of zucchini or cucumber, for example, are a favorite of many loricariid catfish. Ideally, use organic vegetables if possible. You will need to remove any left uneaten before the end of the day with a net, so only offer a single slice at a time.

must know

If you work irregular hours or are going on vacation, do not try feeding your fish more food than usual, because this will have a catastrophic impact on the water quality in the tank. You can invest in an automatic fish feeder, which feeds the fish regularly at predetermined times. Alternatively, slow-release food blocks for vacation use are available, and these will provide the fish with a constant source of food but without the risk of ruining the water quality in the tank.

Diseases

There are many ways in which diseases can be introduced to an aquarium. By knowing how they occur, you will be better prepared to prevent them—or treat them successfully in the event of an outbreak.

Introducing a sick fish into an aquarium is one way of spreading disease; however, it is not the only one. Harmful microbes may be in the water in which the fish are transported from the store, which is why it is not a good idea to empty the fish with the water into the tank (see pages 48–51). In a typical aquarium, there are a number of organisms that can cause infection, but these usually do not have the opportunity. The fish's immune system is able to fight off these microbes, but if its body is injured in any way, through careless handling or fighting for example, infections, such as fungal disease, will have a greater opportunity to attack.

Stress can also play a part in disease, and this helps to explain why fish can often become ill following a move, which is generally one of the most stressful times for a fish. Similarly, an individual that is repeatedly bullied in a tank will probably develop minor scale damage, which will leave the fish susceptible to fungal attack.

Keeping a separate tank

In most cases, the sooner that the signs of illness are observed and the quicker you take action, the easier it will be to treat the fish successfully. You can invest in a small, lightweight acrylic tank to use as a "hospital" tank to isolate and treat sick individuals. It can also serve as a quarantine tank, to be used to house new fish before introducing them to the established tank. When they are moved to the main aquarium, the newcomers will need to integrate within the existing group of fish, and this is often stressful for them at first. However, if you have kept and fed them well for a couple of weeks beforehand, health problems are far less likely to arise during this period.

Combating a power cut

In the case of tropical fish, there will be an increased risk of illness if the fish become chilled, because this depresses their ability to fight off any potential infection. If the electricity goes off, take steps to minimize the effects on the fish.

Instead of adding hot water to try to maintain the temperature, unplug the lights and cover the tank with a duvet or heavy blanket to try to retain as much heat as possible. When the power is restored, allow the temperature to rise again gradually, removing the duvet or duvet before reconnecting the lights. This method is less stressful for the fish.

Keep a close watch on the fish for a few days. The loss of power will affect the filtration system, effectively cutting off the oxygen supply. This may have an impact on the water quality.

Symptoms and diseases

Always check the fish in the aquarium every day for any signs of illness. You should begin any necessary treatment as soon as possible to lessen the risk of secondary infections.

If most of the fish in the aquarium die suddenly, this is more likely to be the result of environmental factors, such as a toxic spray entering the aquarium, which is often drawn into the tank through the air pump. Avoid using such products in the room where the aquarium is sited, because many of them, including flea treatments, are deadly to fish, although they may be safe for other pets.

Parasites and fungus

▶ White spot: Tiny white spots appear over the fish's body. These ulcerate, releasing more of the microscopic, free-swimming, infective tomites to attack other susceptible fish. An affected fish is also at risk of fungal attack. *Use a store-bought remedy to destroy the tomites and watch for signs of fungus.* Common.

▶ Velvet disease: Most often occurs in anabantoids. The disease causes the fish's body color to become yellowish-gray. The fish will rub itself to relieve irritation, and it may display signs of breathing difficulty. *Treat with a store-bought remedy.* Relatively common.

▶ Flukes: These can attach to the skin or less conspicuously in the gills, resulting in labored gill movements. *Store-bought treatments are available, but there is a possibility of reinfection.* Relatively common.

You should avoid purchasing fish that have clamped fins, such as this platy (*Xiphophorus maculatus*). It is often a sign of gill fluke.

▶ **Hole-in-the-Head**: This is most likely to occur in discus, but it can also strike other fish. Whitish spots appear on the head and start to ulcerate. Secondary infection can occur. *Treatment with a drug called miconazole gives the best hope of recovery. Fish that recover may show signs of scarring.* Relatively common.

▶ *Saprolegnia* **fungus**: An infection that strikes after an injury, causing a white haloed effect over the affected area. Infective spores are in the water. *It can be treated directly with a cream carefully applied to the affected area, or by baths with a store-bought remedy. Improve the water quality, and raise the water temperature slightly to improve the fish's immune response.* Common.

The long fins on guppies are susceptible to nips and bites from other fish. Fin damage can often be followed by fungal infections.

Bacterial

▶ **Fin Rot**: This often strikes following damage to the fins and results in reddening of the damaged areas. The risk is greatest if the water quality is poor. There is a also serious risk of secondary fungal infection. *Treat the fish with a store-bought remedy.* Common.

▶ **Mouth fungus**: Guppies and other live-bearers are the most vulnerable fish. The fungus causes an unpleasant cottonwool-like growth in the mouth, preventing the fish from eating—the fish will show signs of weight loss. *It can be treated with an antibiotic bath. Carry out a partial water change in the main aquarium.* Less common.

▶ **Vibriosis**: There are several serious, generalized signs of infection, including reddening of the body, changes in color and swollen abdomen and eyes. It is

Don't purchase a bloated fish, and never buy any fish from an aquarium with white spot (see page 175)—even if only one fish has signs of it. White spot can be spread by the water to another tank.

rapidly fatal and spreads quickly through an aquarium.
It is hard to treat, but antibiotics may help.
Less common.

▶ **Piscine tuberculosis**: There is a chronic loss of weight and color, and the eyes may protrude abnormally. There will be widespread losses in the aquarium. *Note*: Piscine tuberculosis can cause a skin infection in people, although it does not attack their respiratory system.
No treatment possible. Strip down the tank, disinfect it, and then restock it.
Less common.

Viral

▶ **Lymphocystis**: Most likely to be seen in goldfish, but it can strike other fish too. Isolated white nodules will form on the body surface. It is disfiguring but causes the fish little discomfort.
Treatment is not really possible.
Common.

▶ **Malawi bloat**: A problem that affects cichlids from Lake Malawi, especially vegetarian species. The abdomen becomes abnormally swollen and the eyes may protrude—a condition referred to as exophthalmia. It may be caused by a viral infection, possibly associated with a lack of fiber in the fish's diet.
No direct treatment is possible, but adding fiber to the fish's diet may help.
Less common.

▶ **Iridiovirus**: Body color of affected fish darkens noticeably, with the abdomen swellling. It affects many fish.
No treatment possible.
Less common.

want to know more?

Take it to the next level...

▶ **Setting up and maintaining your tank** 38–55
▶ **Fish profiles** 56–165

Other sources...
▶ **Specialized aquatic centers:**
To purchase a quarantine tank and medicines for the fish and for advice on caring for them

▶ **Internet sources:**
Do a search for fish diseases

▶ **Aquatic societies:**
Seek advice on caring for sick fish

2 Breeding

Breeding fish in the home can provide
an intriguing new aspect to keeping fish.
While some fish will breed readily, others
will present a much greater challenge.
If you are hoping to breed your fish, be
prepared to invest in another tank and
further equipment for this purpose. It is
also important to think about how you
will find homes for the extra fish, because
some pairs can produce amazingly large
numbers of offspring.

Breeding behavior

Fish have a number of different breeding strategies, but broadly they can be divided into live-bearing and egg-laying fish. Look out for signs of breeding behavior—there are also measures you can take to encourage breeding.

Live-bearing fish, as their name suggests, give birth to live young, although there is often no direct connection internally between the body of the female and her developing offspring. The eggs may be retained in her body, with the young hatching as they are born. Mating among live-bearers is internal. Perhaps surprisingly, live-bearers display no parental instincts, which means that their young are at risk of being cannibalized from the moment of birth.

In contrast, a number of egg-laying fish are dedicated parents. Various male anabantoids build special nests for their eggs and guard their young when they hatch. Others, such as angelfish, carefully deposit their eggs and will remain in the vicinity of their nest site until the fry emerge, which they will then try to keep safe from predators.

In certain species, the parent fish may even take the eggs into their mouth—this is known as mouth-breeding. They retain the eggs without

A male live-bearer channels his milt, or sperm, into the female's body via a modification of his anal fin, which forms a tubelike structure called the gonopodium.

feeding until the young emerge up to three weeks later. Even then, their parental instincts do not cease—the young fish may retreat back into the relative safety of the mouth of the adult fish if danger threatens. Such behavior is seen in various groups, including bettas and cichlids and a few catfish. Some fish, such as

For most egg-laying fish, the males fertilize the eggs as they are laid by the females. The eggs tend to drift down among plants or may be swept away on currents.

discus, even produce special mucus on their flanks to nourish their young offspring.

A few fish bury their eggs to protect them. Such behaviour is seen in annual killifish, whose natural habitat of temporary pools dries up, leaving the adult fish to die. Safely entombing their eggs in mud until the rains return allows the next generation to hatch. However, this is a special way of breeding, and most egg-laying fish simply scatter their eggs at random. Some fish, such as barbs and tetras, lay large numbers of eggs because in the wild few survive.

Stimulating breeding behavior

A number of triggers can help to encourage breeding. They include adjusting the water temperature slightly in certain cases, while carrying out more frequent partial water changes, to mimic the effect of the rains, which can encourage breeding in the wild. Increasing the amount of live food in the diet can also have this effect. Certain species of live-bearers are much easier to condition for breeding purposes than others, provided that environmental conditions are favorable.

must know

Signs of breeding behavior are usually clear-cut, with male fish pursuing females more actively and their coloration often appearing to be brighter than usual. Females swell up with their eggs or offspring, with certain specific signs, such as the appearance of the black spot on some live-bearers (see page 129), indicating that a brood is soon likely to be born.

Establishing a breeding setup

The type of breeding setup you'll need depends on the species of fish you want to breed. In most cases, it will be better to have a separate aquarium equipped with spawning sites—and even if you don't, you may need a separate tank for the fry.

Fish that are usually housed in pairs instead of as part of a community aquarium may not need special breeding quarters; however, for most other fish, breeding will be more successful away from other fish in a breeding tank. You'll need to provide suitable spawning sites, such as a piece of slate, or a partially buried clay flowerpot for small, cave-spawning cichlids.

Provide bubble-nest builders, such as Siamese fighting fish and other bettas, with plants floating at the top of the aquarium— these can serve as anchorage points for their nest.

In the case of bubble-nest builders, their spawning tank should have a low water level, with plants at the surface. As in other breeding setups, the aquarium should contain a foam instead of a power filter to ensure that the nest is not destroyed by the current and there is no risk of young fish being sucked into the filtration system via the inlet.

Egg scatterers, such as barbs, need an aquarium designed to prevent them from eating their eggs after spawning. Have a low water level and line the floor of the tank with small marbles. Special short heaterstats are available for breeding tanks that are ideal for a shallow water level. The eggs sink rapidly down to the floor and waft between the marbles, out of reach of the fish. Transfer the adults back to the main tank once they have spawned (but leave the marbles in place—the eggs may stick to them).

Some fish spawn among aquatic vegetation, and these fish will use a special spawning mop placed in the breeding tank as a site for laying their eggs. You can use one in the main tank, although there is then a risk that the fish may decide to spawn elsewhere in the aquarium. Once the fish have spawned, remove the mop with the eggs adhering to it.

Troubleshooting tips

Once a pair of fish has started to breed, they often continue to do so regularly, as frequently as every four to six weeks in favorable conditions. If their first attempt is unsuccessful, you should not have to wait long until they try to breed again. If you find that a particular species is not easily persuaded to spawn, it is important to ensure that the water conditions are optimal. A blackwater extract can be beneficial for tetras (see page 45). Do not expose the eggs to bright light because this may inhibit hatching.

must know

Some of the easier aquarium fish to breed
▶ Guppies and other live-bearers
▶ Goldfish
▶ Corydoras catfish
▶ Dwarf cichlids
▶ Angelfish

Rearing the young

The hatching period for the eggs of many fish is short, lasting little more than 24 to 48 hours. Once they hatch, the young fish, known as fry, will eventually need feeding, and they'll require a special diet that will change as they grow.

When the young fry first emerge they are unlikely to be conspicuous. Instead, they usually rest until they have digested the remains of the yolk sac that nourished them while they were in the egg. Only once they start to become free-swimming should you provide them with food. There are special liquid diets available for the young of both egg-layers and live-bearers, and these have been developed to help the fry through the crucial early days of life.

Fry will grow very quickly and become increasingly active and conspicuous as they develop, but at first they usually stay close to the floor of the aquarium, so provide cover for them there.

Homegrown food

You can also supply additional food by growing cultures of microscopic infusoria. You'll need to set up these cultures in advance of spawning, because they will take several days to develop. Simply add some crushed lettuce to a jar of water, and place it in a well-lit location, such as a windowsill. When the culture turns pink you'll know that you have successfully cultured infusoria. You can use a pipette to put the solution into the rearing tank.

As the young fish grow larger, they will be able to eat larger aquatic creatures—the larval stage in the cycle of the brine shrimp (*Artemia salina*), known as nauplii, is often provided at this stage. You will need to buy the eggs and hatch them at home —special kits are available for this purpose.

Young fish are not good swimmers and need food in close proximity, with a gentle current in their aquarium helping to circulate both the water and food. They may need to be fed small amounts of food up to four times a day.

It is important to keep the eggs in a sealed container to ensure they remain viable. You should first dip the nauplii in dechlorinated water before offering them to the fry to remove any salt deposits.

Rearing tips

As the fish grow older, you can introduce finely powdered flake food to their diet. The offspring of live-bearers will take this at once because they are larger in size than the fry of most egg-laying fish.

Keep a close check on the water quality, because it can deteriorate rapidly, given the profusion of food and high number of young fish. You'll need to carry out partial water changes frequently for this reason, taking care to ensure that the water temperature of the fresh water matches that within the tank.

Be prepared to divide up the fish into groups as they grow, trying to match those of similar size to reduce the risk of cannibalism. Remember that not all young fish are of the same shape as their parents, as in the case of discus (see pages 100-1), and they may also differ in terms of their coloration and patterning. Watch out for any fish that are clearly malformed, with a twisted body perhaps, or missing eyes. These should be removed and humanely destroyed—one method is to put them in the freezer.

want to know more?

Take it to the next level...

▶ **Fish profiles** 56–165
▶ **Keeping your fish healthy** 168–77

Other sources...
▶ Specialized aquatic centers: To purchase special food for young fish and equipment for a spawning tank

▶ Internet sources: Do a search for breeding tips on rearing specific types of fish

▶ Fish-keeping magazines: To keep up to date about fish-keeping issues

▶ Fish shows: Some societies offer regular shows so that you can exhibit fish

Glossary

Acidic A reading on the pH scale that is below 7.0.

Adipose fin A small fin associated with characins, such as tetras, which is located on the back between the dorsal and caudal fins.

Aeration Increasing the oxygen content of the aquarium water, both by improving its circulation and by introducing air directly into the water.

Airstone A device that consists of small holes, allowing air entering the aquarium from an air pump to be broken into a series of smaller bubbles, which improves the oxygenation in the tank.

Algae A large group of microscopic plants, some of which may result in greenish growth appearing on rocks and even aquarium glass.

Alkaline A reading on the pH scale above 7.0.

Anal fin The single fin on the underside of the body of a fish, adjacent to the vent.

Barbels Projections of differing shapes and lengths adjacent to the mouth, seen in various groups of fish, especially catfish.

Biological filter A natural filtration process that relies on beneficial aerobic bacteria to break down waste matter in the aquarium.

Blackwater extract A synthetic product that can be added to aquaria to replicate the water conditions under which fish, such as tetras, often occur naturally. The dark coloration is the result of dissolved tannins in the water, which arises from decaying plant matter.

Brackish water Water that is slightly salty, as occurs at the mouth of estuaries for example, where a river flows into the sea.

Breeding trap A means of housing a gravid live-bearer, who is about to give birth, to prevent her young from being cannibalized.

Brood A collective term referring to the offspring of a pair of fish.

Bubble nest A structure made of bubbles of mucus, created by some male anabantoids and catfish, to provide a refuge for their eggs.

Caudal fin The fin at the end of the fish's body. Also sometimes called the tail fin.

Chemical filtration The use of a chemical component, such as activated charcoal, to remove waste from the aquarium. It will probably remove any medicinal treatments, too.

Community tank An aquarium housing a group of fish of different species that normally get along well together.

Conditioning Making water conditions suitable for the fish. Also, preparing them for breeding purposes, which may include modifying their diet.

Dechlorinator A chemical treatment added to the water to remove chlorine, which is toxic to the fish.

Dorsal fin The front or, more commonly, the only fin that extends a variable distance down the back of the fish.

Fancy The creation of a strain of fish with characteristics, such as shape or color, not seen in that species in the wild.

Filter medium The active filtration components of a filter, through which the water passes in order to purify it.

Fins The means by which fish can swim. Some fins may also be specialized to form sensory feelers, such as in many anabantoids, or as a copulatory organ, which occurs in guppies and various other live-bearers.

Flake A type of fish food that is thin and will float on the water surface; it is also easily powdered through the fingers.

Fry Young fish that are newly hatched or born.

Gills The structures located on each side of the head, behind the eyes, through which gaseous exchange can be carried out.

Gonopodium The copulatory organ, derived from a modified anal fin, seen in many different live-bearers, such as guppies.

Gravid A female whose body has become swollen, due to the presence of eggs or young, indicating that she will soon be spawning or giving birth.

Greenstuff Vegetables that are green, such as lettuce or cabbage.

Hard water Water that contains a high percentage of calcium or magnesium salts—the higher the level of salts, the harder the water.

Heaterstat A combined heater and thermostat unit used to regulate the water temperature in the aquarium.

Hybridization The mating of two different species of fish together.

Hydrometer An instrument used to measure specific gravity, giving an indication of the salt level in brackish water.

Infusoria Microscopic food particles, which are the first food of many fry.

Labyrinth organs The organs close to the gills, allowing anabantoids to breathe atmospheric air directly.

Lateral line The sensory device, in the form of a jellyfilled canal, which runs down each side of the fish's body.

Length The size of a fish, measured in a straight line along the body from its snout to the base of the caudal fin.

Live-bearer A fish that gives birth to live offspring instead of laying eggs that hatch later.

Live foods Invertebrate foods used for fish, which may be either aquatic or terrestrial in origin.

Mechanical filtration A way of screening water to remove solid waste matter from it.

Milt The spermatozoa and seminal fluid of a fish; also his testis.

Morph A naturally occurring color variant of a fish, found in a particular area of its range in the wild. It applies especially to cichlids.

Mouthbreeder A fish that hatches its eggs in its mouth—this behavior is especially associated with African cichlids and some anabantoids.

Mulm Solid waste matter, such as decaying plant matter, which can accumulate on the floor of an aquarium.

Mutation A variation that occurs in the coloration or appearance of a fish, which is caused by a genetic change.

Nauplii The larvae in the life cycle of brine shrimp, which are important in the diet of many young aquarium fish.

Nitrogen cycle The natural process that results in nitrogenous waste, in the guise of ammonia, being modified to nitrite, then nitrate before being recycled through nature.

Nuchal hump The swelling seen on the head of some male cichlids.

Operculum The flap on each side of the head covering the gills.

Parasite An organism that lives on the body of another, usually causing harm.

Pectoral fins The paired fins positioned on each side of the body, behind the gills.

Pelvic fins The paired fins lying further back on the body, in front of the anal fin.

pH A measure of the relative acidity or alkalinity of a water sample, with pH7.0 being neutral.

Photosynthesis The process whereby plants use light energy for nutritional purposes, utilizing carbon dioxide and releasing oxygen as a byproduct.

Power filter A self-contained filtration unit, which includes a pump to draw water through the media.

Prepared foods Foods specially formulated to provide fish with a balanced diet.

Reverse osmosis A means of softening hard water.

Rotifer A tiny aquatic organism with cilia, used as a first food.

Scales The protective body covering of most fish.

Siphon The process of removing water from the aquarium by using a tube.

Soft water Water, such as rainwater, that does not contain significant amounts of dissolved calcium or magnesium salts.

Spawning The way in which eggs are laid and fertilized.

Spermatopodium The notch present in the anal fin of some male live-bearers, which enables them to transfer sperm directly into the female's body, resulting in internal fertilization.

Substrate The floor covering in the aquarium.

Swim bladder The buoyancy organ of a fish, which may also provide additional oxygen into the bloodstream.

Tubercles The small swellings on the operculum and pectoral fins, indicating that a male goldfish and related cyprinids are ready to spawn.

Ventral fins The alternative name sometimes used for the pelvic fins.

Water conditioner A product that not only removes chlorine-based products from tap water, but may also give the fish some protection against minor skin infections, too.

Yolk sac The area of the egg that provides food for the developing fry and also nourishes it for a short time after hatching takes place.

Need to know more?

There is a wealth of further information available for fish keepers, particularly if you have access to the Internet. Listed below are just some of the resources that you might find useful while keeping fish.

Fish-keeping organizations

American Cichlid Association
www.cichlid.org

The American Killifish Association
www.aka.org

American Livebearer Association
www.livebearers.org/

Angelfish Society
www.theangelfishsociety.org

Boston Aquarium Society
www.bostonaquariumsociety.org

Canadian Association of Aquarium Clubs
www.caoac.on.ca

Circle City Aquarium Club
www.circlecityaqclub.org

Goldfish Society of America
www.goldfishsociety.org

Greater Chicago Cichlid Association
www.gcca.net

International Fancy Guppy Association
www.ifga.org

International Goby Society
gobiidae.com/int_goby_soc.htm

Long Island Aquarium Society
www.liasonline.org

Marine Aquarium Society of Los Angeles County
www.maslac.org

Pacific Coast Cichlid Association
www.cichlidworld.com

Potomac Valley Aquarium Society
www.pvas.com

Magazines

Aquarium Fish Magazine
P.O. Box 53351
Boulder, CO 80328-3351
www.aquariumfish.com

Tropical Fish Hobbyist
P.O. Box 427
Neptune City, NJ 07754-9989
www.tfhmagazine.com

FURTHER READING

Alderton, David *Encyclopedia of Aquarium & Pond Fish*
(Dorling Kindersley London, UK, 2005)

Alderton, David *Cichlids*
(Bow Tie Press, Irvine, USA, 2003)

Alderton, David *Bettas & Gouramis*
(Bow Tie Press, Irvine, USA, 2004)

Alderton, David *Livebearers*
(Bow Tie Press, Irvine, USA, 2004)

Andrews, Chris *A Fishkeeper's Guide to Fish Breeding*
(Salamander Books, London, UK, 1986)

Andrews, Chris, Excell, A. and Carrington, N. *The Manual of Fish Health*
(Salamander Books, London, UK, 1988)

Axelrod, Herbert R., Burgess, Warren E., Pronek, N., and Walls, J.G. *Dr Axelrod's Atlas of Freshwater Aquarium Fishes*
(T.F.H. Publications, Neptune, USA, 1985)

Burgess, Warren E. *Coloured Atlas of Miniature Catfish: Every Species of Corydoras, Brochis and Aspidoras*
(TFH Publications, Neptune, USA, 1992).

Dawes, John *Livebearing Fishes: A Guide to Their Aquarium Care, Biology and Classification*
(Blandford, London, UK, 1991)

Dawes, John *Complete Encyclopedia of the Freshwater Aquarium*
(Firefly, Ontario, Canada, 2001)

Hieronimus, Harro *Guppies, Mollies, Platys—A Complete Pet Owner's Manual*
(Barron's, New York, USA, 1993)

Konings, Ad *Cichlids from Central America*
(TFH, Neptune, USA, 1989)

Konings, Ad *Cichlids and all the Other Fishes of Lake Malawi*
(TFH, Neptune, USA, 1990)

Scheurmann, Ines *Aquarium Plants Manual*
(Barron's, New York, USA, 1993)

Scott, Peter W *A Fishkeeper's Guide to Livebearing Fishes*
(Salamander Books, London, UK, 1987)

Smartt, J. and Blundell, J.H. *Goldfish Breeding and Genetics*
(TFH Publications, Neptune, USA, 1996)

Index

The numerals in bold refer to the main entries.

Index

Acknowledgments

Most of the photographs in this book were taken at Maidenhead Aquatics (www.fish-keeper.co.uk), Amwell Aquatics (High Rd., Thornwood, Epping, Essex, UK), Israquarium Ltd. (St. Albans Rd., Watford, UK), or Swallow Aquatics (Harling Rd., East Harling near Thetford, Norfolk, UK). We are very grateful to the staff there for their help.

With special thanks to Jeremy Gay and also to Marion and Michael Dent.